# FOCUS ON THE FUTURE

# FOCUS ON THE FUTURE
## A Career Development Curriculum for Secondary School Students

CRSO

Nancy Perry
Zark VanZandt

**INTERNATIONAL DEBATE EDUCATION ASSOCIATION**

NEW YORK * AMSTERDAM * BRUSSELS

Published by

# international debate education association

400 West 59th Street / New York, NY 10019

Library of Congress Cataloging-in-Publication Data

Perry, Nancy, 1934-
 Focus on the future : a career development curriculum for secondary school students / Nancy Perry, Zark VanZandt.
    p. cm.
 ISBN 1-932716-13-0 (alk. paper)
    978-1-932716-13-9

 1. Career education--Curricula. 2. Career education--Study and teaching (Secondary) 3. Vocational guidance. I. VanZandt, Zark. II. Title.

 LC1037.P37 2005
  370.11'3--dc22

                        2005010907

Design by Hernan Bonomo
Printed in the USA

IDEBATE Press Books

# . Contents

## Unit Three: Career Planning: How Do I Get There?

# PART I
## Teacher's Guide

ᮯᮯᮯ

# Overview

This curriculum guide assists teachers in introducing career development into classrooms of students ages 14 to 18. The curriculum has been designed to provide a flexible framework for classroom-based efforts. Teachers are encouraged to adapt and/or integrate the curriculum to meet their needs. They are also urged to add lesson plans and activities, add or update background information, and suggest additional ways to work with parents and the community. Because cultural differences will probably occur, changes to fit into the students' cultural framework are also encouraged.

Before you begin the curriculum, you should become thoroughly familiar with the concepts of career development and its importance to young people today. This guide attempts to provide enough background information for lessons and activities to help you feel confident in teaching the concepts of career development. Each session builds on the knowledge and/or skills taught in the previous lessons. Therefore, you should follow the curriculum in a sequential order.

## How to Use *Focus on the Future*

*Focus on the Future* is divided into two parts: Teacher's Guide and The Curriculum.

**Part I:** Teacher's Guide lists teaching objectives and/or student outcomes. It defines career development and explains the foundations on which modern practice is built. The Guide describes the career-building concepts that direct and illustrate the curriculum and establishes the importance of career development in every student's life.

The Guide also suggests effective teaching strategies based on adolescent characteristics, gives an overview of the curriculum, and explains how each lesson is formatted. Finally, it describes how to construct student portfolios.

**Part II:** The Curriculum is divided into three units containing a total of 36 sessions. Each unit assists students in answering a question essential to their career development.

> **Unit One** helps the student to answer the question "Who am I?" Self-knowledge includes such areas as student interests, abilities, values, and aspirations.
>
> **Unit Two** helps the student to answer the question "Where am I going?" Career and occupational exploration are the basis for this section.
>
> **Unit Three** helps the student to answer the question "How do I get there?" This section guides the student through the decision-making process into actual educational and career-planning.

This Teacher's Guide and The Curriculum will take you step by step through the process of helping your students to think about their futures while making informed decisions to realize their dreams. You are their guide on the wondrous journey to adulthood. Enjoy the journey and know that you are important to their lives now and in the future.

## Student Goals

As a result of participating in this career development curriculum, students will:

1. Understand what career development is.

2. Appreciate the importance of thinking about and planning for their future.

3. Know that they have choices in choosing their lifework.

4. Understand the need for a solid education.

5. See how the behaviors and attitudes they are developing now may affect their future.

6. Learn about themselves and what is important to them.

7. Explore the world of work and make preliminary choices of occupations to investigate.

8. Understand that planning and preparation for the future begin now.

9. Learn how to access resources to help them reach their goals.

10. Know that career development is a lifelong process.

# CAREER DEVELOPMENT

## WHAT IS CAREER DEVELOPMENT?

Career development is an ongoing process that allows individuals to take information they know about themselves, organize it, and use it to learn about the world of work and how they relate to it. The process usually begins very early in life when small children are asked, "What do you want to be when you grow up?" This tells children two things: that they will be something and that they have a choice. Family, community, school, and national events all have an impact on the pathway pursued and the choices made. Career development does not stop when we become employed. We continue to grow and to change, and so does the world around us. The rapidly shifting complexities of the early 21st century demand new ways of looking at our lives. Therefore, the career development process continues throughout a lifetime.

There are opportunities within the career development process to intervene with guidance that helps direct and enhance the process. *Focus on the Future* is such an intervention. It takes the students step by step through activities that will help them make informed career decisions. Career guidance is planned and sequential and should be facilitated by those who are trained to deliver such a program.

Just as the world is changing, so have the definitions we associate with career development. In this curriculum, the following definitions apply:

- **Job:** a position with specific duties and responsibilities in a particular place.

  Example: I have a job teaching mathematics at the Central Secondary School.

- **Occupation:** a field of study or similar group of jobs.

  Example: My occupation is teaching.

- **Career:** the sequence of occupations and other life roles that combine to express one's commitment to work in his/her total pattern of self-development. This concept recognizes that our "jobs" don't exist in isolation from the rest of our lives. We don't leave our lives behind in the morning when we go to work, and work is only one part of our life/career.

  Example: I am a parent and spouse who has chosen to be a teacher.

- **Career-building:** the management of the many events and roles in life that shape our life/career. Some of them we can control (e.g., education and relationships) and some of them we cannot (e.g., the economy, technological change).

  Example: I took the appropriate courses and passed the necessary exams to become certified as a teacher. I enjoy my work but I have been offered an opportunity to do research. Therefore, I am considering a career change.

## THEORIES OF CAREER DEVELOPMENT AND DECISION-MAKING

There are basically two classes of career development theory: structural and developmental.

**1. Structural theories** focus on matching individual characteristics to occupations that mesh with the individual's interests and aptitudes.

- One example of this kind of theory is the **Trait and Factor Theory** developed by Frank Parsons. This theory involves a three-step process in which individuals:

    1. gain a clear understanding of their abilities, interests, resources, limitations, and other qualities;

    2. investigate the requirements and conditions of success, opportunities, and prospects in different lines of work; and

    3. through reasoning, connect these two groups of facts.

- John Holland's **Theory of Vocational Personalities and Environments** is another example of a structural theory. Holland believes that people's occupations are manifestations of their personalities; that people in the same occupation have similar personality characteristics; and people and work environments can be classified into six categories of vocational personalities and environments. These personality and environmental typologies are:

1. **Realistic:** people who prefer to work with things, tools, and/or animals rather than data or people. Farmers, skilled trade workers, and engineers typify this group of people.

2. **Investigative:** people who prefer using intelligence and abstract reasoning in disciplined inquiry, data-gathering, and analysis rather than working with people or things. Scientists, highly specialized technicians, and mathematicians typify this group of people.

3. **Artistic:** highly creative people who concentrate on originality, self-expression, and intuition. They may work with tools to create original works or they may work with people through their expressive media. Writers, artisans, and performers typify this group of people.

4. **Social:** people who prefer working with people rather than working with things or data. Counselors, social workers, teachers, and hospitality workers typify the people in this group.

5. **Enterprising:** people who seek and enjoy leadership and persuasion of others for purposes of accomplishing organizational, political, or financial goals. Salespeople, supervisors, and politicians typify the people in this group.

6. **Conventional:** people who enjoy working with data more than people or things. Accountants, financial workers, and clerical workers typify this group of workers.

## HOLLAND'S SIX PERSONALITY TYPES

- REALISTIC
- INVESTIGATIVE
- ARTISTIC
- SOCIAL
- ENTERPRISING
- CONVENTIONAL

Holland assumes that while no one is exclusively described by one personality type, most people can be typed by a combination of three related personality types. For example, a farmer may be realistic (R), conventional (C), and investigative (I). The Holland Code would be RCI. This code is related to a number of different but similar work environments.

2. **Developmental theories** are based on the premise that individuals throughout life go through developmental stages that influence their choice of work.

   • Donald Super's **Developmental Self-Concept Theory** focuses on career as a lifelong process during which an individual's vocational self-concept develops through five stages: growth, exploration, establishment, maintenance, and decline. He bases his theory on 14 propositions that emphasize career maturity, self-concept, and multiple life roles.

---

### SUPER'S FIVE DEVELOPMENTAL STAGES

• **GROWTH (BIRTH–14):** In the later stages, individual thinks about interests and abilities.

• **EXPLORATION (15–24):** Individual begins articulating a self-concept, narrowing down fields and career choices, and ultimately finding a job or getting into a final training program.

• **ESTABLISHMENT (25–44):** Individual becomes committed to occupation and moves up in the field.

• **MAINTENANCE (45–64):** Individual rides out career and might shift attention to family.

• **DECLINE (65–):** Individual plans for retirement and then retires.

---

## SUPER'S FOURTEEN PROPOSITIONS

1. People differ in their abilities, personalities, needs, values, interests, traits, and self-concepts.

2. People are qualified, by virtue of these characteristics, for a number of occupations.

3. Each occupation requires a characteristic pattern of abilities and personality traits, with tolerances wide enough to allow for some variety of occupations for each individual.

4. Vocational preferences and competencies, the situations in which people live and work, and, hence, their self-concepts change with time and experience.

5. This process of change may be summed up in a series of life stages characterized as a sequence of growth, exploration, establishment, maintenance, and decline.

6. The nature of the career pattern (occupational level attained and the sequence, frequency, and duration of trial and stable jobs) is determined by the individual's parental socioeconomic level, mental ability, education, skills, personality characteristics, and career maturity.

7. Success in coping with the demands of the environment relates to career maturity—a constellation of physical, psychological, and social characteristics.

8. Career maturity is a hypothetical construct.

9. Development through the life stages can be guided, partly by facilitating the maturing of abilities and interests and partly by aiding in reality-testing and in the development of self-concepts.

10. The process of career development is essentially that of developing and implementing occupational self-concepts.

11. The process of synthesis or of compromise between individual and social factors, between self-concepts and reality, is one of role playing and of learning from feedback.

12. Work satisfactions and life satisfactions depend on the extent to which the individual finds adequate outlets for abilities, needs, values, interests, personality traits, and self-concepts.

13. The degree of satisfaction people attain from work is proportional to the degree to which they have been able to implement their self-concepts.

14. Work and occupation provide a focus for personality organization for most men and women, although for some persons this focus is peripheral, incidental, or even non-existent.

Source: Momberg, Christine. 2005. The Relationship between Personality Traints and Vocational Interest in a South African Context. Master's thesis, University of Pretoria.

- John Krumboltz's **Social Learning Theory** emphasizes three main forms of learning experiences:
  1. Reinforcement: Focuses on the rewards one gets from certain behaviors. Behavior is influenced by both positive (praise, money) and negative reinforcers (threats, punishment).
  2. Modeling: People also learn by modeling, i.e., observing others directly or indirectly (TV, reading).
  3. Instrumental learning/conditioning: Classical conditioning refers to learning by associating ordinary or environmental events with previous experiences.

Krumboltz believes that because interest and decision-making skills are learned, providing experiences through a coordinated career guidance program will help to expose individuals to a number of options that can influence their career decision-making. Furthermore, since career decision-making is a learned process and because it is similar to decision-making in non-career areas of life, decision-making should be taught as a skill that can be used in all areas of life. Since modeling is such a potentially strong form of learning, career development facilitators need to provide direct and vicarious opportunities for positive modeling in a wide variety of career opportunities.

There are many other theories concerning how people make life and career decisions. This curriculum draws from both classes of theories in that students are encouraged through activities to identify and classify their knowledge of themselves and explore the various occupations that might match their characteristics, while understanding that there is not just one occupation or "perfect job" for each person and that, through time and experience, we change. The curriculum emphasizes decision-making as a valuable life skill and encourages modeling and mentoring as a powerful learning strategy.

## GUIDING PRINCIPLES OF CAREER-BUILDING

The Human Resource Department of Canada has identified five career-building principles that have been especially effective in working with young people. Instead of focusing on THE BIG DECISION, young people are encouraged to look at THE BIG PICTURE of their life.

**1. Change Is Constant.** One night of listening to international news can convince us that our world is changing at an unprecedented rate. Therefore, we need a fluid approach to career-planning. We need to recognize that we don't make ONE BIG DECISION; that decision-making is a continuous process. We make decisions in many ways—some without thinking about them, others by weighing the pros and cons, still others by whether they "feel right" to us.

We need to recognize as well that we may change our decisions as our circumstances change. We make the decision that seems to be the best one for us at the time. In any choice, there's an upside and a downside. We pass up some opportunities but, in return, we gain other experiences.

**2. Learning Is Ongoing.** When we recognize that the world is constantly changing and that many of the jobs of the 21st century have yet to be invented, it becomes apparent that both learning and career-building must be ongoing, lifelong processes. It is equally as important to "learn to learn" as it is to learn specific content material. Continuous learning uses both formal study skills as well as other creative modes.

3. **Follow Your Heart.** It is important for us to explore and to come to know where our "heart" and values lie. Yet traditional messages such as "make the right decision," "play it safe," or "be realistic" often discourage us from exploring and maintaining an awareness of our dreams.

We need to learn to trust ourselves. Fear of failure prevents us from making mistakes and, therefore, learning from them. In an ever-changing world in which flexibility and adaptability are essential, we need to encourage individuals to take calculated risks and teach them how to do this.

4. **Focus on the Journey.** The journey, not the destination, becomes the focus of our personal meaning. Given the changing nature of our world, choosing an occupational destination and doggedly pursuing the goal may end up being a limiting and meaningless experience. The goal may not exist by the time we reach it, and other possible goals may have emerged. We need to establish broad visions of the future that set a general direction, but not a specific target. Our life situations tell us where we should focus our greatest energy. Sometimes we have to deal with our immediate needs in taking exams, making car payments, etc. At other times, we're able to meet some of our more enduring needs—strong relationships, work that we value, etc. But for ongoing life/career satisfaction, we strive to satisfy both our immediate needs and our enduring needs.

5. **Access Your Allies.** Value is often placed on our ability to be strong and independent. Although these may be good qualities, we often find that "we can't do it alone." In each aspect of our life/career, we need the help and support of people we trust. These people are our allies—they can be family members, friends, co-workers, fellow students, bosses. They can be all ages and come from all walks of life. They share the common element of having our best interests at heart. They can help in decision-making and networking with others who may be helpful to us.

---

### FIVE GUIDING PRINCIPLES OF CAREER-BUILDING

- **CHANGE IS CONSTANT**
- **LEARNING IS ONGOING**
- **FOLLOW YOUR HEART**
- **FOCUS ON THE JOURNEY**
- **ACCESS YOUR ALLIES**

---

## WHY CAREER DEVELOPMENT IS IMPORTANT TO STUDENTS

### The Changing Workplace

There is no doubt that the workplace is changing throughout the world. In those countries moving from a planned economy to a market economy, the change is even more dramatic. Even in countries that have long been operating in a market economy, the rules have changed. Technology has given birth to a new type of workplace—and workforce.

Manufacturing, or producing goods, is giving way to the service industry. Machines can now do repetitive tasks, and machines do not take vacations or sick leave and can work 24 hours a day. Improved transportation and technology have reduced worldwide communication to seconds. With the ability to produce goods anywhere and to move them, competition is now global.

## The Changing Workforce

Your students will be competing for jobs with more than just other candidates in your area. They will be competing with the Chinese and Canadians and Peruvians. In order to compete globally, companies are "re-engineering" to cut costs while becoming more efficient and effective. One way employers are doing this is by adopting work styles that are different than the traditional employer-employee relationships. Many are contracting with individuals to work on a fee-for-service basis rather than on a salary. Many are hiring individuals to work part time rather than a full workweek. Some people share jobs, and others work from their homes via telecommunications. In most cases, workers will be selling a service—and the service is the knowledge and skills of the individual. Even those in traditional employer-employee relationships are finding changed expectations in the workplace. The high-performance workplace requires that all workers be

- responsible for their own actions
- self-motivated
- adaptable
- service oriented
- capable of communicating
- skilled and knowledgeable (both specialized and general)
- entrepreneurial

Are your students ready for this new workplace? Are they willing and able to take the responsibility for managing their own lives? Do they understand the basics of entrepreneurship, service, and communications, as well as reading, writing, and arithmetic? Can they access, interpret, and evaluate data? Do they understand that they must have marketable skills and that the opportunity to prepare is now?

## THE SHIFT FROM OLD TO NEW WORK PLACE

| Traditional Workplace | → | Emerging Workplace |
|---|---|---|
| Authority invested in Supervisor | → | Authority delegated to workers |
| Individual work tasks | → | Work teams, multi-skilled workers |
| Mass production | → | Flexible production |
| Long production runs | → | Customized production runs |
| Company-dependent career | → | Own your own job, skills, career |
| Workers as a cost | → | Workforce as an investment |
| Advancement by seniority | → | Advancement by documenting skills |
| Minimal qualifications accepted | → | Screening for basic skills |
| Minimal training for some workers | → | Training essential for all workers |
| Narrow skills for some | → | Broader skills for all |
| Information to decision makers | → | Information to all |
| Little concern for foreign markets | → | Great attention to foreign markets |
| Worker "classes" by title and degree | → | Workers appreciated by degree of core skills |

Adapted from Feller, Rich, and Gary Walz. 1996. *Career Transitions in Turbulent Times: Exploring Work, Learning, and Careers.* Greensboro, NC: ERIC-CASS.

## THE IMPORTANCE OF CAREER DEVELOPMENT

Today's world requires us to be flexible and adaptable. In our life/career, we can adapt most successfully if we learn to manage change, learn what we love to do, gain the competence required to do it, and trust and appreciate ourselves.

The curriculum through which you will be leading your students will help them to find direction in their lives. It will make education more relevant to their future goals and will be a motivating force for achievement. In the process, they will learn how to make informed decisions and have a better understanding of career development as a lifelong process.

# Effective Teaching Strategies

This curriculum is built around the premise that an individual's career development requires both information and insight. Teachers are accustomed to providing information through lecture and discussion. These teaching strategies will be an important part of this curriculum. However, students need also to reflect on the information and decide how it applies to their unique vision of the future. A facilitative teaching approach using such methods as brainstorming, role-playing, and small group activities is effective in stimulating insight. All of these methods will be discussed.

Students are also going through developmental stages of physical and psychological growth that affect the way in which they learn. For example, adolescents are going through physiological, physical, and psychological changes that cause them to shed the images of themselves as children and to test new identities as emerging adults.

Physiologically, teens are going through hormonal changes of puberty. The body is still developing, although their adult shape is taking form. They take an interest in the opposite sex, and relationships have new meaning. Their moods may go from one extreme to another.

Physically, the adult body image is emerging in both males and females. Unfortunately, growth is seldom steady or consistent. Girls tend to develop more quickly and may look like adults while boys their age may still look gangly. Girls and boys usually want to emulate some ideal body shape that they have seen in the media, movies, or sports. Both sexes are usually very conscious of how they look.

Psychologically, feedback from their peers becomes very important as adolescents shape new concepts of their identities. The older teens are striving for independence, which can sometimes cause friction in the family. They often rebel against traditional thinking and are constantly "trying out" new ideas as they clarify their values. Although belonging to a group is still important, older adolescents are more willing to risk being different.

Teachers cannot reverse the characteristics of adolescence. However, they can take advantage of those features to enhance communication and to make their teaching strategies more effective. The activities in this curriculum allow students to socialize and learn from each other. New ideas are tested in the safety of small groups. Finally, role-playing is an important strategy that allows for trying out new roles without risking rejection from others. The curriculum uses the following teaching methods.

## Teaching Methods[1]

**1. Lecture:** Background information is provided for each lesson. A lecture is a structured and organized presentation of information on a particular topic delivered by the teacher. Although the lecture is a quick way of providing needed information, it also has its

---

1. Adapted from Shapiro, Susan. 1991. Nutrition and Your Health. New York: Open Society Institute.

drawbacks. If lectures are too long and fail to involve the participation of the students, the teaching opportunity may be lost to the restlessness of the recipients.

2. **Discussion:** Discussions represent a verbal interchange between and among the students and teachers. Discussions provide students with the opportunity to share their ideas, feelings, and thoughts about a particular topic. Discussions are particularly helpful in that they enable students to utilize their thinking skills, expand on their own ideas, and hear differing opinions from their classmates. Discussions broaden and deepen students' understanding and give them opportunities to apply what they have learned. Discussion groups, large and small, can be utilized throughout this curriculum.

3. **Brainstorming:** Brainstorming is a very popular teaching technique that encourages the free flow of ideas on a specific topic. The leader presents a problem or life situation to think about and then encourages the students to generate as many solutions and/or alternatives to the problem as possible. In the initial stage of brainstorming, the free flow of ideas is encouraged. All ideas are noted without comment and are evaluated only after the exchange stops. The students are then asked to examine each of the ideas presented.

4. **Role-Playing:** Role-playing is just as the name implies. Students are encouraged to assume a role other than their own in response to acting out a life situation. Each role-play lasts only as long as needed to act out a variety of ways in which the situation could be addressed. Because students are not playing themselves or necessarily expressing their own ideas, it is a safe way in which to explore some difficult situations without threatening the student's privacy. Role-playing is designed to help students explore their feelings, thoughts, and actions in a safe environment. Students should be given the opportunity to volunteer for role-playing and then be taught some techniques to help them with the activity. For example, students can step out of their characters and tell others how they are feeling. They can be assigned "alter egos" who can whisper ideas in their ears when they appear to be stuck. The students may also ask to switch roles with their peers to generate new perspectives on the same situation. Role-playing can provide ample material for discussion and should be fun.

5. **Structured Activities:** A structured activity is any experience that has been planned in advance and is designed to facilitate learning. A structured activity often simulates a life event in a controlled environment so that it can be observed and discussed. The purpose of structured activities is to increase self-understanding in the face of complex life situations.

## TEACHER/STUDENT INTERACTION

Teaching the curriculum is dependent on open lines of communication between and among participants. Students need to understand and utilize basic rules of classroom discussion, while teachers need to understand and utilize some basic interpersonal skills to facilitate group discussion. The following strategies will help students and teachers to communicate effectively.

**Classroom Discussion Rules for Students:** Classroom discussions, presentations, and activities run more smoothly when everyone is aware of the rules and practices them. Rules help students and adults to exercise their rights and to manage their responsibilities. Some examples of useful classroom rules are:

1. **Listen to One Another:** This is accomplished by maintaining eye contact with the speaker and not talking. When the speaker finishes, the next speaker gives a brief overview of what the previous person has said before sharing his/her ideas.

2. **Speak One at a Time:** Only one person may speak at a time during a group discussion. It is sometimes useful to have the speaker hold a symbol of authority, such as a gavel or a key, that is passed on to the next speaker. This says to all the students that this person now has the floor and should be listened to. If other students carry on private conversations, stop the discussion until the designated speaker has everyone's full attention. Listening to one another and speaking one at a time are two rules that reinforce each other.

3. **Stay on the Topic:** Sometimes students will wander from the main point of discussion. Rather than criticize them for doing so, the group leader can say: "I'm not sure how this relates to what we are talking about. Can you help me?" This gives the student a chance to make the point clearer or to recognize that the discussion is not appropriate.

4. **Everyone's Ideas Are Important:** Students need to be encouraged to share. Every student in the class has value and should feel free to express feelings or thoughts. Let the students know that their ideas are valuable and are appreciated. If a student states a myth or false statement, respond by saying something like, "Many people would agree with you. However, we now know that. . . ." In this way, the student does not have to experience shame or ridicule for an incorrect response.

5. **Right to Pass:** All students are encouraged to participate in classroom activities and discussions. However, a student should have the right to pass in those situations when participating might be embarrassing.

6. **Outlaw Putdowns:** Self-expression is more likely to occur when students understand that it is okay to disagree with someone, but that it is not appropriate to attack or ridicule other people for their ideas. Help students to understand what putdowns sound like and how others feel when this type of behavior takes place. Let students know that such behavior is unacceptable and will not be tolerated.

7. **Questions Are Valued:** Actually, there are no dumb questions. Every question has value. Let students know that all of their questions will be respected and answered throughout the curriculum.

**Interpersonal Skills for Leaders:** Bringing out key ideas, letting students know that you understand what they are saying, and intervening when students make unclear statements are necessary activities for effective leaders. There are five interpersonal skills that, when applied, can help leaders to facilitate helpful communications between and among participants. The skills to which we refer are listening, reflecting, clarifying, questioning, and seeking examples.

1. **Listening:** Listening is an action-oriented activity that requires the collective utilization of the listener's senses in response to the behavior of another person. Leaders can improve their ability to listen by paying attention to both verbal and nonverbal cues of students.

2. **Restating:** Restating is the process of repeating almost verbatim what another person has said. While restatement should be used sparingly, it provides leaders with an opportunity to make sure that they have heard the student correctly. If the message was misunderstood, the student now has the chance to restate the desired response. Restating can also be used to let the student know that the message was received by the leader.

**3. Clarifying:** Clarification goes beyond restating what a student has said. It allows leaders some latitude in connecting a number of the student's thoughts in the formation of a new concept or understanding. In doing so, a leader might say, "During class you made the following point about ___. Let me see if I understand you correctly?" The student now has the chance to agree or disagree with the new thought or idea that has been advanced. Clarification helps students and leaders to develop new understanding of a topic.

**4. Questioning:** When a leader is trying to understand a student's thoughts on a topic, the use of questions can be very helpful. When questions are used, they should be used sparingly and with caution A few tips on how to use questions effectively follow:

- Ask open-ended questions. "Could you tell me more? How did you feel? Is there anything else that you wish to say?"

- Ask only one question at a time. Allow students to answer the question asked before going on to others. Too many questions may create confusion.

- Give the student an opportunity to answer the question. Some people require time to think through a response before answering. Allow sufficient time if you believe that the student is internally formulating an answer.

- Validate the student's response. Acknowledge the student's response by thanking him/her for participating. If incorrect information is provided, be positive with the student and then introduce the correct information.

- Give the student an out. When asking questions, watch for signs of agitation, fear, or an inability to respond. Intervene after a few moments of silence and say, "You seem to be giving a lot of thought to my question. Would you like more time or would you like some help with the question?"

- End on a positive note. End questions and responses on a positive note. Let students know that your questions were not easy and that they did a good job sharing their ideas.

**5. Seeking Examples:** Students often find it easier to provide examples or illustrations when trying to convey an abstract concept or idea. Merely asking "Could you give me an example or describe what you are trying to say?" will help students advance their thoughts.

All five interpersonal skills used in conjunction with one another are designed to help students expand on and develop their ideas. These communication skills keep conversations flowing. They can be used during classroom discussions, in activities, during role-plays, and in generating alternatives during decision-making.

---

## FIVE INTERPERSONAL SKILLS TO FACILITATE COMMUNICTION

- LISTENING
- RESTATING
- CLARIFYING
- QUESTIONING
- SEEKING EXAMPLES

## Group Dynamics

All groups, large or small, go through stages of development. The stages are forming, storming, norming, and performing. When a new group is formed, the participants are generally kind to each other and act with respect. However, as the business of the group becomes apparent, there typically will be disagreements and unease. Know that this is a normal part of group development and that the group will usually work out its standards, or norms, and will finally reach a level of productivity or performing. However, in the dynamics of any group, there will be certain variables that the leader will have to address. Having a plan in advance helps the leader to be more effective. Some variables are:

- **Development of subgroups:** Subgroups represent small clusters of students that form over time when they are allowed to select their own groups in which to participate. Maintaining the same subgroups may be helpful in that students develop a level of comfort that allows them to risk more and to derive support from their peers. However, as students become more familiar with each other, they may also be less inclined to follow the rules. One way of handling the subgroup issue is to form a variety of groups, varying their size and composition.

- **Opposing Groups:** Group members may divide into separate camps based on opposing points of view. When this happens, encourage the group to be accepting of each other's positions. Help the students to understand that it is okay for people to disagree with one another, but that it is not okay to be disagreeable. Focus on the issues instead of the positions. Provide the members with an opportunity to discuss their feelings and to identify solutions to their problems.

- **Blaming:** Blaming occurs when students openly attack individuals or subgroups for specific difficulties occurring in their group. Blaming can be very divisive in that it breaks down trust, impedes progress, and isolates individuals. Once you notice it, do not allow blaming to continue. Stop the process and remind the students that such activity will not be tolerated. Blaming can become a teachable moment where students can apply the communication skills they have been learning to resolve their own conflicts.

- **Monopolizing:** Some students are so eager to participate that they take over the session. When that happens, acknowledge the person's contributions, but also be direct and indicate that you want to give everyone a chance to be involved. Break eye contact with the monopolizer and reduce the number of times that you call on this student.

- **Inappropriate sharing:** If students, in their eagerness to share, begin to discuss personal or very sensitive material about themselves or about family members that you believe should be discussed privately, step in immediately. Do so in a kind way, acknowledging the feelings of the student, but suggesting that this conversation should take place with you after the session.

- **Silent members:** Many students tend to be rather quiet. They may feel more comfortable opening up in smaller groups and do so with an invitation from other group members. However, just because group members remain silent does not necessarily mean they are not learning or are uninterested in what is taking place. Some students learn best by being quiet and observing. Be ready to reach out to these youngsters, but also acknowledge their right to be quiet if that is what they choose.

- **Side conversations:** During large group discussion, a small number of students may be carrying on their own conversation, which is a distraction to the group. Stop the process and invite these students to share their conversation with the entire group.

Let them know that the class is not able to benefit from their ideas nor are they able to hear what the others are saying. Review the ground rules for group discussion and move on.

- **Failure to stick with the topic:** Occasionally, a group member has something to express that is not related to what is being discussed in the group. Again, stop the process and ask the student how what he or she is saying relates to the topic the group is discussing. This gives the student an opportunity to re-explain or to acknowledge that the topic is unrelated to the focus of discussion. Tell the student to either discuss the point with you privately or to bring it up again when the present discussion comes to a close.

- **Group discomfort:** Sometimes leaders may sense some discomfort or a dynamic occurring in the group, but are unable to identify what may be happening. When this occurs, the leaders should acknowledge their feelings with the group and ask for their input. For example, a leader may say, "The group seems very quiet today. Can you help me understand what is happening?"

Most groups function very well, and the students look forward to discussions and activities that pertain to their futures. However, the leader needs to keep a pulse on the dynamics of the group and be sensitive to group needs. This will enhance the conditions of the learning environment and make it easier for the students to address their needs while learning what is being taught.

# ABOUT THE CURRICULUM

This curriculum has been designed to be user-friendly. The information you need for each activity is contained within the lesson plan. However, in Unit Two, it will be important to use other resources to help students with current labor market information available in your area. If you do not have a governmental department responsible for providing this information, use your daily newspapers or other media to analyze the trends. Labor market information is all around us. We just need to open our ears and eyes to its importance.

Because career development is a growth process and very individual, it is recommended that students not be graded. The passing or failing, or more likely, the participation or non-participation of students, will hurt only them. They should understand that the results of their efforts can affect their future and the responsibility is on them to make the most of it. They are being offered an opportunity to learn about themselves and how their academic and vocational development will affect their ability to live the lifestyle they would like for themselves. We cannot control all the events that affect occupational choice. However, it is always better to plan and give direction to our efforts. David Campbell wrote a book entitled, *If You Don't Know Where You Are Going, You Will Probably End Up Somewhere Else* (Ave Maria Press, 1990). This might be the theme for educational and career planning.

A test of career development knowledge is included at the beginning of the curriculum. You can use this both before and after completing the curriculum to measure the knowledge gained by your students. It is useful both as an individual measure of growth and as a group measure. You can see which areas may need more reinforcement and which lessons are well learned. Students should be aware that they will be given a chance at the end of the curriculum to show how much they have progressed in knowledge about career development and thus in making important decisions about their future. The ultimate indicator of success for students at this age will be an understanding of the opportunities available to them as adults and the preparation needed to pursue the pathway of their choice.

This curriculum is divided into three units. Each unit helps the student to answer one of the critical questions of career development.

- **Unit One: Self-Knowledge** helps the student to answer the question, "Who am I?" What are my interests, abilities, values, and aspirations and how do I relate them to occupational choice?

- **Unit Two: Career and Educational Exploration** helps the student to answer the question, "Where am I going?" What are the opportunities available to me after I have finished my formal education? What are different occupations really like and how might I find out more about them?

- **Unit Three: Career Planning** helps the student to answer the question, "How do I get there?" What educational and occupational preparation is required to pursue the career of my choice? What do I need to do to make my vision a reality?

At the beginning of each unit, there will be background information applicable to the lessons presented. Teachers are urged to use other available information to enhance the lessons. However, the background information presented will suffice to answer most questions.

There are twelve sessions m each unit. Each session is divided into activity and discussion portions. The sessions are broken down further into key instructional elements:

- OVERVIEW
- DURATION
- (Learning) OBJECTIVES
- MATERIALS NEEDED
- PREPARATION
- (Step-by-Step Guide to the) ACTIVITY
- DISCUSSION

Most sessions also include a number of suggested discussion questions and one or more optional activities. Lesson durations are given as suggestions only. You should allow for teachable moments when an expansion of the lesson seems advisable. The program is designed to be as flexible as possible, so that you can use your creativity, experience, and knowledge to adapt it to the class, taking into account students' personalities, home-life situations, and relevant events in the community.

Parents are the first teachers of their children and will exert the most influence on their career choice. Therefore, it is vital that parents be encouraged to follow their children through the curriculum and to be open to their questions and discussions. We have included an appendix: A Parent's Guide to Career Decision-Making, which you may give to parents to help them understand what you are trying to accomplish and how they can become involved.

Icons are used throughout the curriculum to alert you to certain tasks. They are:

|  | Students will put the work in their portfolios. Distribute the portfolios at the beginning of the activity and collect them at the end of the class for use in future lessons. |
|---|---|
|  | Students will share work with adults at home/community. |
|  | Homework assignment. Read following session to see what is expected. |

At the end of each unit, there is a checklist of competencies that students should have attained as a result of participating in the activities. This is meant to be a self-assessment that will serve as benchmarks for students' progress and an individual way for students to identify areas in which they may need more help.

If you gave the test of career development knowledge at the beginning of the program, you should repeat the same assessment at the end to serve as a measure of individual student growth and identification of group strengths and weaknesses.

# STUDENT PORTFOLIO

## WHAT IS A PORTFOLIO?

A portfolio is both a place and a process. It is a place for students to keep their work as they are guided through the career development process. It helps students to see their progress over time and to reflect on the meaning of the curriculum experiences in their lives. Although the portfolio is an important student record, it is different from other educational records in that the student owns it. It documents the thinking of students as they go through the career development process and can be referred to in the future. The student portfolio should contain the best and most current work of the student. Therefore, as students mature and change, they can change the work in their portfolios. At the end of the program, the portfolio should be given to the student to be kept for future use.

## HOW ARE THE PORTFOLIOS CONSTRUCTED?

Students should use a file folder as the cover of their portfolio. The cover should have the name of the student under the title Focus on My Future.

### FOCUS ON MY FUTURE
### John Doe      Grade 11

Other information, such as teacher's name, can be added as desired. Students should be encouraged to decorate their portfolios to fit their personalities.

Use pieces of colored paper to divide the portfolio into four parts. Label each part:

**Unit One: Who Am I?**

**Unit Two: Where Am I Going?**

**Unit Three: How Do I Get There?**

**My Career Plan**

In the curriculum, students will be asked to complete many forms and to provide information about themselves. Most of this work will go into their portfolios.

 When you see this icon in the lesson plan, tell the students that this work will go in their portfolios. Keep the portfolios at school until the end of the curriculum to assure availability.

# PART II
# The Curriculum

ଔ৪ৡ

# • UNIT ONE: SELF KNOWLEDGE
## Who Am I?

| | | |
|---|---|---|
| | Session 1 | Introduction to Focus on the Future Pre-Test |
| | Session 2 | When I'm Thirty |
| | Session 3 | Dream Analysis |
| | Session 4 | The Life Clock |
| | Session 5 | Interest Inventory |
| | Session 6 | Skills Inventory |
| | Session 7 | Work Values |
| | Session 8 | Managing Time |
| | Session 9 | Gender Stereotyping |
| | Session 10 | Understanding Strengths |
| | Session 11 | Putting It All Together |
| | Session 12 | Interviewing |
| | Competency Checklist for Unit One | |

# UNIT ONE: SELF KNOWLEDGE
# WHO AM I?

This unit will help students analyze their interests, abilities, talents, work values, and aspirations. Students should understand that all work has value. However, each of us is unique and may follow different pathways to work that is satisfying. You may have decided to become a teacher because of a desire to help others, work with young people, or shape lives, or maybe because the work hours and days suited your lifestyle. You also may have become a teacher because you were influenced by family or friends, or because it was the only profession available to you at the time. Perhaps you really wanted to be an artist or a doctor.

When we were young, each of us dreamed of a possible future—a future in which we were respected or revered for our talents. Even though we might not have fulfilled that dream, it was still important as a clue to the person we wanted to be. This unit will help students to discover that person through a series of activities in which the student is encouraged to dream and to analyze that dream. However, we do not develop in isolation. Our environment and events that we cannot control impact the choices we make. As we grow older our experiences affect our decision-making, if we have family responsibilities, we must consider them as well as ourselves. The choice often becomes a compromise with reality. However, for our students, it is a time to dream and to explore and discover themselves and the world around them.

After an introduction to the process of career development and the program, sessions help students consider the importance of this process in their lives. You should stress that this program is not just another subject to get through. It is an opportunity for students to think about themselves and the future they would like to have. It is a time to think about the preparation needed to attain their desired work and consider the reality of the options open to them. However, students should not be discouraged from pursuing their dreams. Strong motivation can often overcome obstacles. Students should understand that there will not always be someone to guide them, and they will need to know how to make important decisions. This is their life. What students get out of the program will depend on what they put into it.

This unit begins by explaining the guiding principles of career development and the terminology that is used. Then students are asked to dream about their futures, to analyze those dreams and, finally, to look at the decisions that must be made and the reality of the world we live in. Students then have the opportunity to define their interests, analyze their skills and talents, and think about what they want to get from their work, i.e., their work satisfiers. Leisure time activities can give clues to the complete personality and how everything we do contributes to our well-being. Students learn time management as a means to bring balance into their lives. They also become aware of attitudes and stereotyping that keep people from following their dreams. Finally, they look at what they have already achieved in life and what they have learned about themselves. In the final activity of the unit, students must articulate their self-knowledge in an interview for their ideal job.

# SESSION 1:

# INTRODUCTION TO *FOCUS ON THE FUTURE* AND PRE-TEST

## OVERVIEW

Students are introduced to *Focus on the Future* and a number of key definitions. They will complete a questionnaire that measures their baseline understanding of the world of work and career development.

## DURATION

Approximately 1 hour

## OBJECTIVES

Students will learn the foundation concepts and terminology that will be used throughout the program.

## MATERIALS NEEDED

Discussion Rules
What I Know About the World of Work (copies for each student)
Three Foundation Terms resource sheet (copies for each student)
Five Guiding Principles resource sheet (copies for each student)
Master List of Occupations activity sheet (copies for each student) (optional)
colored paper to act as dividers in the portfolio
file folder
pencil or pen

## PREPARATION

Prepare a summary of *Focus on the Future* for delivery to students. Stress the importance of knowing one's interests, abilities, and values in thinking about a career. Additionally, one must know what is available in terms of occupational choice and how to prepare for that choice.

Consider preparing, in advance, posters of the key terms (job, occupation, career) and the five guiding principles:

- Change is constant.
- Learning is ongoing.
- Follow your heart.
- Focus on the journey.
- Access your allies.

# ACTIVITY

1. Introduce students to *Focus on the Future* by describing the program. It is important to give them a sense of what they'll be participating in over the next several weeks. Make students aware that they are about to embark on a career exploration journey. To succeed on their journey, they will have to take responsibility for their choices. Therefore, it is important that they learn as much as possible about themselves and how their uniqueness relates to career choice. They will also need to face the reality of available options and the preparation needed to reach career goals. This will be done in phases beginning with the dream for their future and then facing the realities of life.

2. Distribute Discussion Rules and explain that these rules will be guiding the class.

3. What I Know About the World of Work, which students will complete individually, without assistance, and hand in. The questionnaire will be completed a second time at the end of the program and compared with this set of results, allowing an assessment of how well the program's objectives have been met. Filling out the questionnaire at this point establishes a benchmark for each student.

4. Upon completion, go over the correct answers (available on the teacher's sheet) with students. Don't know answers are considered incorrect. Tell students that they will learn more about these statements in the curriculum.

5. Have students construct a portfolio according to the directions given on page 21. Explain that throughout the program students will be keeping their papers in this portfolio. At the end of the program, it will offer documentation of their work and be a reminder of the activities that they have done. The questionnaire will be the first item to put in the portfolio and should be inserted under "Unit One: Who Am I?"

6. Distribute and introduce Three Foundation Terms resource sheet. Students should be able to distinguish between these terms early in the program, but they may need to be revisited regularly until they can grasp the differences. Have students include the handout in their portfolios for future reference.

7. Distribute and discuss Five Guiding Principles resource sheet. The five principles, created by the Human Resource Department of Canada, are incorporated throughout this program as a way to illuminate the objectives of *Focus on the Future*. They help students reflect, in an ongoing manner, on the relevance of the program's activities to real life and on the changing nature of the world of work. Tell students to include the handout in their portfolios for future reference.

8. Collect the portfolios for further classroom use.

# DISCUSSION

1. What changes have you noticed recently at school? What changes in your neighborhood?

2. What useful things have you learned outside of school?

3. What surprises have you experienced that turned your life in a direction you weren't expecting?

4. Who has helped you make an important decision?

# OPTIONAL ACTIVITY

Students may start a master list of occupations they encounter during the program. Keep it posted at all times and encourage students to add to it whenever they learn of a new occupation, including ones they come across outside of the program: at home, on TV, in movies or books, on the radio, in newspapers, in community activity, or on travels. You may want to alphabetize the listing to avoid duplication of entries.

# DISCUSSION RULES

1. **Listen to One Another:** Maintain eye contact with the speaker and listen to what he/she is saying. When the speaker finishes, the next speaker should give a brief overview of what the previous person has said before sharing his/her ideas.

2. **Speak One at a Time:** Only one person may speak at a time during a group discussion. Do not interrupt a speaker or talk during his/her presentation.

3. **Stay on the Topic:** Sometimes people wander from the main point of discussion. Rather than criticize someone for doing so, say: "I'm not sure how this relates to what we are talking about. Can you help me?" This gives the person a chance to make the point clearer or to recognize that the discussion is not appropriate.

4. **Everyone's Ideas Are Important:** Everyone in the class has value and should feel free to express feelings or thoughts. If you think someone is presenting a myth or making a false statement, respond by saying something like this: "Many people would agree with you. However, we now know that. . . ." Never shame or ridicule a person for an incorrect response.

5. **Right to Pass:** You are encouraged to participate in the classroom activities and discussions, but you have the right to pass in those situations when participating might be embarrassing.

6. **No Putdowns:** You can disagree with someone, but it is not appropriate to attack or ridicule other people for their ideas. Putdowns are unacceptable and will not be tolerated.

7. **Questions Are Valued:** There are no dumb questions. Every question has value. We must respect and answer all questions.

# WHAT I KNOW ABOUT THE WORLD OF WORK
## (STUDENT EDITION)

NAME:_____

DATE:_____

| NUMBER | STATEMENT | AGREE | DISAGREE | DON'T KNOW |
|---|---|---|---|---|
| 1. | Only people who make more than $30,000 a year pay income tax. | | | |
| 2. | Parents who work can afford to buy almost everything their children want. | | | |
| 3. | Women can make excellent plumbers. | | | |
| 4. | Finishing high school has no connection to how much money you can earn. | | | |
| 5. | The terms *job* and *career* mean the same thing. | | | |
| 6. | Transferable skills are skills you can pass on to your co-workers. | | | |
| 7. | The amount of leisure time you have depends on your occupation. | | | |
| 8. | Hating your high-paying job is no reason to leave it. | | | |
| 9. | You should start thinking about working life now. | | | |
| 10. | Improving technology sometimes creates jobs and sometimes takes them away. | | | |
| 11. | Once you graduate from a university or college, the classroom part of learning is over. | | | |
| 12. | Math skills are only useful in scientific or technical work roles. | | | |
| 13. | The jobs available today aren't much different from the ones your parents had. | | | |
| 14. | Anyone with a job can afford to buy or rent a house. | | | |
| 15. | Volunteering can give you skills that can help you get a job. | | | |

| Number | Statement | Agree | Disagree | Don't know |
|--------|-----------|-------|----------|------------|
| 16. | If you lose your job, you may have to retrain before you can work again. | | | |
| 17. | When you have a job, it's easy to save money for the things you want. | | | |
| 18. | Men and women are equally suited to scientific and technical work roles. | | | |
| 19. | The best occupations to pick are the ones that pay the most money. | | | |
| 20. | If you're smart and leave school before graduation, you'll get to the good jobs ahead of your classmates. | | | |
| 21. | What you study in high school can affect your job choices later in life. | | | |
| 22. | Gross monthly income is the money left over after you pay your bills. | | | |
| 23. | When you have a job, you can take a great vacation every year. | | | |
| 24. | When you're choosing among career options, it's good to talk to people who have jobs that appeal to you. | | | |
| 25. | You should take your personality into account when you choose an occupation. | | | |
| 26. | Most people will have several different jobs during their careers. | | | |
| 27. | Lifelong learning applies to teachers and trainers, but not to other adults. | | | |
| 28. | How much money you can make is the most important factor in choosing an occupation. | | | |
| 29. | Changing technology can affect whether or not you can keep your job. | | | |
| 30. | If you work hard and do your best, you will never lose your job. | | | |
| 31. | Because you will spend a big part of your adult life working, you should play now. | | | |

| Number | Statement | Agree | Disagree | Don't know |
|---|---|---|---|---|
| 32. | You will have to learn and build skills all your life to keep working in jobs you like. | | | |
| 33. | Your job description tells: what you do, where you work, and how many hours you work each week. | | | |
| 34. | One person losing a job doesn't affect other people in a community. | | | |
| 35. | Balancing your budget means that you never spend more than you earn. | | | |
| 36. | When you have a job, you can buy what you want. | | | |
| 37. | Dreaming is important to career-planning. | | | |
| 38. | There really aren't many occupations or many jobs to choose from. | | | |
| 39. | Job satisfaction is affected by the hours you work, the place you work, the people you work with, and the things you do. | | | |
| 40. | Unless you're rich, starting a business is never a realistic career possibility. | | | |
| 41. | Education and work will take up most of your adult life. | | | |
| 42. | Sex role stereotyping is a guide to the best job. | | | |
| 43. | One of the good things about earning lots of money is that you always have lots of time to enjoy it. | | | |
| 44. | Nursing is the perfect career choice for some men. | | | |
| 45. | If you have a good education, and work hard, you'll be guaranteed to get the job you want and keep it for the rest of your life. | | | |
| 46. | The most appropriate time to start exploring and planning your career is your last year in school. | | | |
| 47. | The only kind of intelligence that matters is how smart you are in school. | | | |

*Source:* Baran, D. *The School-Work Project Survey.* Developed for the National Life/Work Centre, Memramcook Institute, New Brunswick, Canada.

# WHAT I KNOW ABOUT THE WORLD OF WORK
(TEACHER EDITION)

NAME:_____

DATE:_____

| NUMBER | STATEMENT | AGREE | DISAGREE | DON'T KNOW |
|--------|-----------|-------|----------|------------|
| 1. | Only people who make more than $30,000 a year pay income tax. | | X | |
| 2. | Parents who work can afford to buy almost everything their children want. | | X | |
| 3. | Women can make excellent plumbers. | X | | |
| 4. | Finishing high school has no connection to how much money you can earn. | | X | |
| 5. | The terms *job* and *career* mean the same thing. | | X | |
| 6. | Transferable skills are skills you can pass on to your co-workers. | | X | |
| 7. | The amount of leisure time you have depends on your occupation. | X | | |
| 8. | Hating your high-paying job is no reason to leave it. | | X | |
| 9. | You should start thinking about working life now. | X | | |
| 10. | Improving technology sometimes creates jobs and sometimes takes them away. | X | | |
| 11. | Once you graduate from a university or college, the classroom part of learning is over. | | X | |
| 12. | Math skills are only useful in scientific or technical work roles. | | X | |
| 13. | The jobs available today aren't much different from the ones your parents had. | | X | |
| 14. | Anyone with a job can afford to buy or rent a house. | | X | |
| 15. | Volunteering can give you skills that can help you get a job. | X | | |

| Number | Statement | Agree | Disagree | Don't know |
|---|---|---|---|---|
| 16. | If you lose your job, you may have to retrain before you can work again. | X | | |
| 17. | When you have a job, it's easy to save money for the things you want. | | X | |
| 18. | Men and women are equally suited to scientific and technical work roles. | X | | |
| 19. | The best occupations to pick are the ones that pay the most money. | | X | |
| 20. | If you're smart and leave school before graduation, you'll get to the good jobs ahead of your classmates. | | X | |
| 21. | What you study in high school can affect your job choices later in life. | X | | |
| 22. | Gross monthly income is the money left over after you pay your bills. | | X | |
| 23. | When you have a job, you can take a great vacation every year. | | X | |
| 24. | When you're choosing among career options, it's good to talk to people who have jobs that appeal to you. | X | | |
| 25. | You should take your personality into account when you choose an occupation. | X | | |
| 26. | Most people will have several different jobs during their careers. | X | | |
| 27. | Lifelong learning applies to teachers and trainers, but not to other adults. | | X | |
| 28. | How much money you can make is the most important factor in choosing an occupation. | | X | |
| 29. | Changing technology can affect whether or not you can keep your job. | X | | |
| 30. | If you work hard and do your best, you will never lose your job. | | X | |
| 31. | Because you will spend a big part of your adult life working, you should play now. | | X | |

| Number | Statement | Agree | Disagree | Don't know |
|--------|-----------|-------|----------|------------|
| 32. | You will have to learn and build skills all your life to keep working in jobs you like. | X | | |
| 33. | Your job description tells: what you do, where you work, and how many hours you work each week. | X | | |
| 34. | One person losing a job doesn't affect other people in a community. | | X | |
| 35. | Balancing your budget means that you never spend more than you earn. | X | | |
| 36. | When you have a job, you can buy what you want. | | X | |
| 37. | Dreaming is important to career-planning. | X | | |
| 38. | There really aren't many occupations or many jobs to choose from. | | X | |
| 39. | Job satisfaction is affected by the hours you work, the place you work, the people you work with, and the things you do. | X | | |
| 40. | Unless you're rich, starting a business is never a realistic career possibility. | | X | |
| 41. | Education and work will take up most of your adult life. | X | | |
| 42. | Sex role stereotyping is a guide to the best job. | | X | |
| 43. | One of the good things about earning lots of money is that you always have lots of time to enjoy it. | | X | |
| 44. | Nursing is the perfect career choice for some men. | X | | |
| 45. | If you have a good education, and work hard, you'll be guaranteed to get the job you want and keep it for the rest of your life. | | X | |
| 46. | The most appropriate time to start exploring and planning your career is your last year in school. | | X | |
| 47. | The only kind of intelligence that matters is how smart you are in school. | | X | |

*Source:* Baran, D. *The School-Work Project Survey.* Developed for the National Life/Work Centre, Memramcook Institute, New Brunswick, Canada.

# THREE FOUNDATION TERMS

**Job:** a distinct position with specific duties and responsibilities in a particular place. For example, photographer at the department store in Centerville.

**Occupation:** a cluster of jobs with common characteristics requiring similar skills. For example, photographer.

**Career:** the combined total of all the events in one's life and how they relate to the work one chooses. This includes education, work, family, leisure activities, and more.

# FIVE GUIDING PRINCIPLES

## CHANGE IS CONSTANT

We change constantly, and so does the world around us—including the working world. Because the skills of a single occupation will no longer take workers from the beginning to the end of their working lives, adaptability is an important skill to carry into the next century.

## LEARNING IS ONGOING

Graduating from high school or college does not signal the end of learning. Opportunities to learn are everywhere, just waiting to be recognized and taken advantage of.

## FOCUS ON THE JOURNEY

Traveling through life is like traveling down a road: having a destination gives direction, but most of the time is spent moving along. Pay attention to the journey, with all its pitfalls, sidetracks, opportunities, and highways to new destinations.

## FOLLOW YOUR HEART

Dreaming can lead to an understanding of what we really want. And what we really want is a prime motivator in shaping a rewarding career. It may take a lot of work to attain it, but never be afraid to pursue a dream.

## ACCESS YOUR ALLIES

The journey of life is not taken alone. Friends, family, teachers, neighbors—any of them can be inspiring and helpful allies when it comes to judging what steps to take on life's path.

# MASTER LIST OF OCCUPATIONS

1._____    11._____

2._____    12._____

3._____    13._____

4._____    14._____

5._____    15._____

6._____    16._____

7._____    17._____

8._____    18._____

9._____    19._____

10._____   20._____

# SESSION 2:
# WHEN I'M 30

## OVERVIEW
Students will think and write about what they imagine their lives to be like when they are 30.

## DURATION
Approximately 30 to 40 minutes

## OBJECTIVES
Students will begin to identify and clarify their values and aspirations.

## MATERIALS NEEDED
A Day in My Life in My 30th Year assignment sheet

writing materials

## PREPARATION
The teacher should have a list of writing prompts for the students.

## ACTIVITY
1. Hand out A Day in My Life in My 30th Year assignment sheet. Tell students that they are going on an imaginary trip into their futures. Ask them to imagine waking up on a spring morning in their 30th year. They are to let their dreams surface and not try to fit them into the world as it is now. Have them answer each question on the assignment sheet.

2. Have students write a description of a day in their lives when they are 30 years old based on their answers to the questions.

   *Note:* Although this may be used as a writing exercise, the content is more important than the grammar or spelling.

## DISCUSSION
1. What will the world be like in 2035?

2. What forms of transportation will exist?

3. What kind of clothes will be worn?

4. What will schools be like?

5. What new occupations will exist?

## OPTIONAL ACTIVITY

Instead of having the students write a paper, have them make a collage using pictures from magazines and newspapers.

# A DAY IN MY LIFE IN MY 30TH YEAR

1. Imagine waking up one morning when you are 30 years old. Answer the following questions on a separate piece of paper:

    a. Where are you living (town, city, neighborhood, country)?

    b. What kind of housing do you have (apartment, house, cottage)?

    c. Who lives in this place with you (parents, spouse, children, relatives, friends)?

    d. How do you dress for work (work clothes, casual, professional, uniform)?

    e. What are your working hours (dawn to dusk, nine to five, etc.)? Are the hours regular or do they change from day to day?

    f. Where do you work (office, store, factory, outdoors, indoors)? Do you travel from place to place in your work?

    g. How do you get to work (walk, bus, car, motorcycle, plane, boat)?

    h. What kind of work are you doing (writing, problem-solving, working with machines, computers, people)?

    i. Who do you work with (workers on assembly line, by myself, a few other people)?

    j. What kind of lunch do you have (bring own, eat at company cafeteria, eat at restaurant, go home for meal)? Do you eat with other people or by yourself? What kind of supervision do you have at work?

    k. At what time do you arrive home after work?

    l. What kind of leisure time do you have?

    m. What do you enjoy doing in your leisure time (playing sports, reading, collecting, hiking, watching movies, etc.) What equipment do you need (stereo, sailboat, motorcycle, bicycle, camera, computer, horse)?

    n. What was the most important thing that happened in this day?

2. On a separate piece of paper, write a description of a day in your life when you are 30 years old based on the answers to these questions.

# SESSION 3:
# DREAM ANALYSIS

## OVERVIEW

In small groups, students will share their papers written in the previous class. They will ask others to analyze their dream of the future focusing on the lifestyle, kind of job, and surroundings. What does this tell them about the values and aspirations of that student?

## DURATION

Approximately 30 to 40 minutes

## OBJECTIVES

1. Students will consider what is important to them in their work and lifestyle.
2. Students will begin to make connections between their aspirations and their preparation.

## MATERIALS NEEDED

A Day in My Life in My 30th Year essays (prepared in the previous lesson)

Dream Analysis activity sheet (each student should receive the same number of sheets as members in his group)

Dream Weekend activity sheet (copies for each student)

## PREPARATION

Students must complete their essays from Session 2 and bring them to class.

## ACTIVITY

1. Assemble students in groups of 3 or 4 and distribute enough copies of Dream Analysis activity sheet so that each student has the same number of sheets as members in his/her group. Have each group complete the sheet.

2. When all students have had a chance to share their stories, reassemble the class and ask students what they learned from this exercise? Were they surprised? Did they have a role model in mind when they created their situation?

3. Have the class complete Dream Weekend activity sheet.

## DISCUSSION

1. Ultimately, our decisions are based on our values or what is important to us. Ask the students to think about their values now. Do they think those will be their values when they are 30?

2. What influences might make a difference in the choices they make?

## OPTIONAL ACTIVITY

Have students interview adults about the dream they had of their future when they were the age of the students. Did they achieve their dream? Why or why not?

# DREAM ANALYSIS

## Instructions:

1. Ask one member of your group ("the reader") to read his/her "A Day in My Life in My 30th Year" essay aloud.

2. Write your answers to the following questions and discuss them with the members of your group.

3. Ask the reader to either affirm or disagree with the group's analysis and check the appropriate box.

## DREAM ANALYSIS

### READER'S NAME:_____

| STATEMENT | AGREE | DISAGREE |
|---|---|---|
| What does this essay tell you about the reader's interests? | | |
| What are some things that are important in his/her work? | | |
| Is this dream possible? | | |

# DREAM WEEKEND

What kind of story would you write if it were the weekend or your leisure time.

• How would you spend your unstructured time?

• Would you be alone or with someone else?

• Would you need special equipment such as a vehicle?

• What does this tell you about yourself?

# SESSION 4:

# THE LIFE CLOCK

## OVERVIEW

Students complete a Life Clock, noting past and future benchmarks in their lives. In the process, they will see how much of their lives they will be working.

## DURATION

30 minutes

## OBJECTIVES

Students will be able to visualize their life journey in order to understand the importance of making informed life decisions.

## MATERIALS NEEDED

Life Clock activity sheet (copies for each student)

markers or colored pencils

## PREPARATION

Draw the Life Clock on the board, marking the years. If you choose the optional activity, invite a guest to your classroom to speak to the class.

## ACTIVITY

1. Distribute copies of Life Clock activity sheet and discuss the exercise, explaining that the Life Clock symbolizes a person's lifetime, beginning with birth, and is divided into age segments.

2. Ask students to fill in the Life Clock following the instructions on the activity sheet.

3. Ask students to designate with a color, pattern, or design (e.g., a pie chart) from the point they started school to the completion of their formal education.

4. Ask students to do the same with a different color or design to indicate the portion of their life devoted to full-time work.

5. Tell the students that they may add any other benchmarks that they feel may be important in their lives.

## DISCUSSION

1. How much of your life will be spent working?

2. How much of your life will be spent at school or learning?

3. Do education, work life, and job satisfaction relate to each other? How?

4. Why is it important to enjoy the work you do?

5. How does it feel to dream of and visualize the future? Is it important to dream of the future? Why or why not?

6. Might your Life Clock look different if you redrew it in five years? Why or why not?

## OPTIONAL ACTIVITIES

1. Invite a retired person (or 2 or 3) to the class to share their Life Clocks. Encourage them to discuss how the world has changed and continues to change.

2. Ask the students to take home the completed Life Clocks and invite a parent or other adult to complete their own Life Clock. Have students report on the differences, similarities, and surprises on an adult's Life Clock.

# LIFE CLOCK

**Instructions:**

Indicate the dates of the following benchmarks on the Life Clock, writing a label next to each:

- When you started school

- Where you are now

- When you expect to graduate from high school

- When you expect to start and graduate from college, university, or other training program, and if you are planning on postsecondary education

- When do you expect to start working full time

- When you think you might get married, if you choose to

- When you expect to start a family, if you plan to have children

- If you do plan to have children, when each child will leave home (assume it takes 20 years for a child to become independent)

- How old you will be when you plan to retire from work

**2006 © Open Society Institute**

The Publisher grants permission for the reproduction of this worksheet for non-profit educational purposes only.
Activity sheets may be downloaded from www.idebate.org/focusonthefuture.htm

# LIFE CLOCK

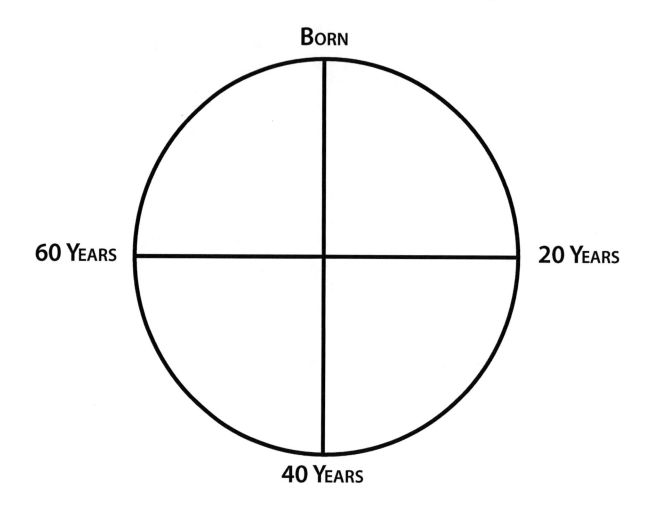

# SESSION 5:
# INTEREST INVENTORY

## OVERVIEW

Students will complete an interest inventory, helping them to think about how their interests are related to possible occupations.

## DURATION

45 minutes

## OBJECTIVES

Students will understand how their interests play a part in career decision-making.

## MATERIALS NEEDED

20 Things I Love to Do activity sheet (copies for each student)

student Life Clocks

Types of Activity resource sheet (copies for each student)

## PREPARATION

None

## ACTIVITY

1. Hand out a copy of the activity sheet to each student and review. In the first column, have students list 20 things they love to do. These might include going to the movies, reading a book, playing a sport, talking with friends, walking in the woods, going to a museum, painting, etc.

2. Have students look at each item on the list and designate whether it is done with other people (P) or alone (A).

3. Ask students to mark the activities that cost more than $20.

4. If students have engaged in this activity in the last month, tell them to mark the "frequency" column.

5. Distribute copies of Types of Activity resource sheet to each student and review.

6. Ask the students to categorize each of their activities by type: data, people, or things.

7. Divide the class into small groups and have students tell what they learned about themselves from this activity.

## DISCUSSION

1. Why is it important to consider your interests when thinking about a future occupation? (Refer to Life Clock.)

2. Do your interests fall into similar types of activity? What does this tell you about your occupational choice?

3. Make a list of possible future occupations using these clues.

# 20 THINGS I LOVE TO DO

## Instructions:

1. List 20 things you love to do.

2. Indicate whether each activity is done with other people (P) or alone (A).

3. Mark the activities that cost more than $20.

4. If you have engaged in this activity in the last month, mark the "frequency" column.

5. Refer to the Types of Activities resource sheet. Categorize each activity on your sheet as either D (working with data), P (working with people), or T (working with things). Do your interests fall into similar types of activity?

6. What kinds of occupations might support your interests?

| ACTIVITY | P(EOPLE)/ A(LONE) | MORE THAN $20 | FREQUENCY* | D(ata)/P(eople) /T(hings)** |
|---|---|---|---|---|
| 1. | | | | |
| 2. | | | | |
| 3. | | | | |
| 4. | | | | |
| 5. | | | | |
| 6. | | | | |
| 7. | | | | |
| 8. | | | | |
| 9. | | | | |
| 10. | | | | |
| 11. | | | | |

| | | | | |
|---|---|---|---|---|
| 12. | | | | |
| 13. | | | | |
| 14. | | | | |
| 15. | | | | |
| 16. | | | | |
| 17. | | | | |
| 18. | | | | |
| 19. | | | | |
| 20. | | | | |

\* Engaged in activity in the last month.

\*\* D=Working with data ideas

P=Working with people

T=Working with things

## POSSIBLE OCCUPATIONS:

1.

2.

3.

4.

5.

# TYPES OF ACTIVITY

**Working with data and ideas:** If you like to work with data and ideas, such as gathering information and facts by reading or performing tests and experiments, you might enjoy work in research. This might lead you to develop new ways to do things or a new product. You might also design, write, or draw to express your ideas.

**Working with people:** If you like to work with people, you may find an occupation in which you teach others by explaining or showing how to do things: giving advice, helping others with their problems, caring for others, persuading others to influence their opinions, or organizing and directing their activities.

**Working with things:** If you like to work with or use machines or tools, you might be happiest in an occupation in which you set up and operate, adjust, or repair them. Drivers of vehicles or machinery also fit into this category.

## SESSION 6:

# SKILLS INVENTORY

## OVERVIEW

By telling a story about a successful experience they have had, students will think about the skills they have already acquired and how they may be related to future occupational choice.

## DURATION

45 minutes

## OBJECTIVES

1. Students will be able to identify skills they have already developed.

2. Students will understand that they can develop skills at school, at home, or in the community.

3. Students will begin to relate skills to future occupational choice.

## MATERIALS NEEDED

Skills Inventory activity sheet (copies for each student)

"The Party"

## PREPARATION

Find or write a story about an unsuccessful event, or use "The Party" below to guide your thinking. Students will analyze the event and think about what skills might have been used to make the event a success.

## ACTIVITY

1. Distribute copies of Skills Inventory activity sheet to each student and review. Ask students to write an account of an event in which they were involved that was successful. This could be planning an event for the family, being recognized at school or in the community for an achievement, etc.

2. Divide the class into pairs. Ask student #1 to read his/her story to student #2. Student #2 should listen for the skills that were needed to make the event a success.

3. Tell student #2 to give feedback to student #1 about the skills noted. Have student #1 comment on these skills and think of other incidents in which these skills were used. Student #1 should list the skills he/she feels confident about.

4. Ask the students to change roles and repeat the procedure.

5. Explain to the class that skills that can be used in many different occupations are called transferable skills. Examples are organizational skills, communication skills, analyzing and synthesizing, etc.

6. Read the class a story about an event that was unsuccessful or use "The Party" below.

7. Ask the students to analyze the skills that might have been used to make this a successful event.


## DISCUSSION

1. What kinds of skills are important in any work (communication, organization, planning, time management, analyzing resources, etc.)?

2. How important are these in potential occupations you have considered?

3. What other kinds of skills are necessary?

# SKILLS INVENTORY

## Instructions:

1. On a separate piece of paper, write an account of a successful event in which you were involved.

2. List the skills that made the event a success, and those that you feel confident about.

| SKILLS THAT MADE FOR SUCCESS | SKILLS I FEEL CONFIDENT ABOUT |
|---|---|
| 1. | 1. |
| 2. | 2. |
| 3. | 3. |
| 4. | 4. |
| 5. | 5. |
| 6. | 6. |
| 7. | 7. |
| 8. | 8. |
| 9. | 9. |
| 10. | 10. |

# THE PARTY

Jane and Bob decided to give a party to celebrate the end of the school year. They were excited about the fun they would have with their friends and could talk of nothing else. Finally, Bob said, "But where will we have the party?"

"Oh, I'm sure we can have it at my place. My parents won't mind," said Jane. "But what about food?"

"I'll pick up something," said Bob.

The day of the party arrived. Spirits were high as Bob rang Jane's doorbell. A quick look at Jane's face made him realize all was not well. "We can't have the party here. My parents are going out for the evening and they say I can't have a party unless they are here."

Bob groaned, "Didn't you ask them ahead of time?"

Jane quickly replied, "Well, they never go out. How was I to know? Maybe we can go to Mary's place. Where's the food?"

"Food? Was I supposed to bring something?" said Bob. At this point Susan arrived. Then Mary. Jane and Bob explained the situation.

"What's for music?" asked Mary.

"Oh we thought that David could bring his tape player," chimed in Jane. "He has great recordings." Just then David arrived, empty handed.

"Some party," Susan muttered. Everyone stood around looking at each other. "Oh well, school is out."

"I just remembered I have to wash my hair," Mary said as she made a quick exit. She was joined by Susan, who said something about her mother. David looked at his watch and said that he had planned only to drop in for a short time anyway.

Bob and Jane looked at each other. "Well, that leaves us," said Bob. "At least we can . . ."

"Not really," Jane replied. "I'm grounded for planning a party without asking my parents' permission!"

# SESSION 7:
# WORK VALUES

## OVERVIEW

It is important for students to realize that there are many factors that go into making work satisfactory. This lesson will help them define what is important to them in the work environment as they choose from a list of work values.

## DURATION

35–45 minutes

## OBJECTIVES

1. Students will become aware of work values.

2. Students will be able to identify the work values most important to them.

## MATERIALS NEEDED

Work Values activity sheet

## PREPARATION

If you are not distributing copies of the Work Values activity sheet to each student, put the list of work values on the board. Be prepared to read the definition for each.

## ACTIVITY

1. Distribute copies of the Work Values activity sheet. Define work values and discuss the importance of selecting work that fits an individual's work values.

2. Ask students to complete the activity sheet. Once the sheets have been completed, review with the class.

## DISCUSSION

1. Consider your work values in relation to the occupations listed that are related to your interests.

2. Consider your work values in relation to the occupations listed that are related to your skills.

3. Do you see a pattern emerging? Are there work values that are so important to you that you would give up the job rather than the value?

## OPTIONAL ACTIVITY

Ask the students to take the list of work values home and talk to their parents about their parents' work values. Have they changed over the years? How?

# WORK VALUES

When selecting an occupation or job, it is important to select one that fits your values. This checklist can help you to identify what is important to you. These work values can bring satisfaction to the work you choose.

## Instructions:

1. Consider each value below. If this value is important to you, put a check mark by it.

2. When the list is complete, go back and identify your 3 most important work values. List them in order of priority.

## WORK VALUES

_____Authority: You control others at the work site.

_____Celebrity Status: You attract immediate notice because you are well-known.

_____Competition: You compete with others at the work site.

_____Creativity: You use your imagination to create new ways to do or say something.

_____Flexible Work Schedule: You have a job that lets you choose your own hours of work.

_____Help to Others: You provide services to people who need help.

_____Independence: You decide for yourself what work to do and how to do it.

_____Influence.: You influence the opinions or decisions of others.

_____Intellectual Stimulation: You have a job that requires a considerable amount of thought and logic.

_____Outside Work: You want to work outdoors.

_____Persuasion: You convince others to take certain actions.

_____Physical Work: You work in a job that requires substantial physical activity.

_____Prestige: You have a job that gives you status and respect.

_____Public Contact: You have a job in which you deal with the public every day.

_____Recognition: You have a job in which you gain public notice and recognition.

_____Research: You search for and discover new facts and apply them.

_____Risk-Taking Work: Your job may require risks—physical or financial.

_____Routine Work: You have a job in which you do the same things repeatedly.

_____Seasonal Work: You are employed only at certain times of the year.

_____Supervision: You direct, manage, or supervise the activities of others.

_____Travel: You are required to take frequent trips in your work.

_____Use of Mathematics: You use mathematics or statistics in your work.

_____Variety: Your duties change frequently.

_____Wealth: You have a job where you can earn a large amount of money.

_____Work with Children: Your job is teaching or caring for children.

_____Work with Your Hands: You work with your hands or hand tools.

_____Work with Machinery: You use machines or other equipment.


## MY 3 MOST IMPORTANT WORK VALUES ARE:

1.




2.




3.

# SESSION 8:
# MANAGING TIME

## OVERVIEW
Students will take the 168 hours in a week and budget how they will use their time.

## DURATION
60 minutes

## OBJECTIVES
1. Students will learn how much time they will have for family, leisure time activities, and normal maintenance of lifestyle.

2. Students will realize that time outside of work is important.

## MATERIALS NEEDED
A Week in My Life activity sheet (copies for each student)

colored pencils or crayons

ruler

## PREPARATION
None

## ACTIVITY
1. Distribute copies of A Week in My Life activity sheet. Ask students to fill in the hours for the essential activities. What remains is the amount of time left for leisure.

2. Have the students convert their figures into a pie chart, choosing a different color or pattern for each category.

## DISCUSSION
1. What did you learn from this activity?

2. Were you surprised at the amount of leisure time available to you each week?

## OPTIONAL ACTIVITY
1. Have students tell how they would use their leisure time each week and how much it would cost.

2. Have students ask their parents how they would fill out the chart.

# A WEEK IN MY LIFE

| ACTIVITY | HOURS x # OF DAYS | HRS. / WK. |
|---|---|---|
| ESSENTIAL ACTIVITIES | _____HRS X 7 = | |
| WORKING | _____HRS X 7 = | |
| TRAVELING | _____HRS X 7 = | |
| PREPARATION | _____HRS X 7 = | |
| SLEEP | _____HRS X 7 = | |
| LAUNDRY | _____HRS X 7 = | |
| SHOPPING | _____HRS X 7 = | |
| REPAIRS AND CHORES | _____HRS X 7 = | |
| CLEANING AND BILLS | _____HRS X 7 = | |
| LEISURE TIME | _____HRS X 7 = | |
| TOTAL HOURS IN A WEEK | | 168 |

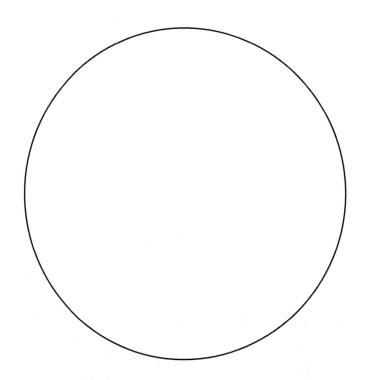

# SESSION 9:
# GENDER STEREOTYPING

## OVERVIEW
Students will explore and discuss their possible biases and preconceptions and how these notions may form barriers to career choice.

## DURATION
35 minutes

## OBJECTIVES
1. Students will be able to recognize stereotypical biases and how they limit choice.
2. Students will expand the options that they can consider as occupational choices.

## MATERIALS NEEDED
Gender Stereotyping activity sheet (one for each group)

## PREPARATION
None

## ACTIVITY
1. Divide students into small groups of 4 or 5. Include a mix of both boys and girls in each group.

2. Distribute copies of Gender Stereotyping activity sheet to each group. Have each group list occupations that they consider to be female occupations and occupations that they consider to be male occupations. They should not judge the lists at this time. They are simply making a list with everyone's suggestions and reasons for suggestions.

3. After they have completed their lists, ask the group to look at each occupation and decide if it could be done by the opposite gender. For example, could a male do a job on the female list? Tell the group to cross out any job that could be done by either gender.

4. Make two columns on the board. Label one female and the other male. Ask each group to list in the appropriate columns the occupations that were not crossed out.

5. Ask each group to comment on any occupations that are listed.

## DISCUSSION

1. Why is it important to consider all occupations as appropriate for either male or female?

2. Compare the wages of occupations considered predominantly male or female.

3. Remember the career-building principle: follow your heart. How might that be applied to gender stereotyping?

4. How can gender stereotyping limit choices?

## OPTIONAL ACTIVITY

Invite workers in nontraditional occupations (e.g., a female in a predominantly male occupation) to visit the class and to talk about the choice they made and what it has meant to them.

# GENDER STEREOTYPING

## Instructions:

1. List occupations that are female and occupations that are male.

2. Look at each occupation and decide if it could be done by the opposite gender. Cross out those jobs that could be done by the opposite gender.

| MALE OCCUPATIONS | FEMALE OCCUPATIONS |
|---|---|
| 1. | |
| 2. | |
| 3. | |
| 4. | |
| 5. | |
| 6. | |
| 7. | |
| 8. | |
| 9. | |
| 10. | |
| 11. | |
| 12. | |
| 13. | |
| 14. | |
| 15. | |
| 16. | |
| 17. | |
| 18. | |
| 19. | |
| 20. | |

# SESSION 10:
# UNDERSTANDING STRENGTHS

## OVERVIEW

Students will be introduced to psychologist Howard Gardner's Seven Intelligences. This activity will help them to define their strengths in relation to career choice.

## DURATION

45 minutes

## OBJECTIVES

1. Students will identify their strengths.

2. Students will understand how their strengths and achievements are linked to possible occupations.

## MATERIALS NEEDED

Gardner's Seven Intelligences (copies for each student)

## PREPARATION

None

## ACTIVITY

1. Distribute copies of Gardner's Seven Intelligences to each student and review. Read the definitions of the seven intelligences. Explain that all types of intelligences are used in life. Most of us can identify which intelligences are our strengths and which are our weaknesses. As you reach each definition, have students list possible occupations related to that type of intelligence.

2. Organize the class into small groups and ask each group to create activities for each of the seven intelligences on the topic of "pollution." The following are examples:

   - Word Smart: Write articles about pollution in their town.

   - Number Smart: Research the causes and amounts of pollution.

   - Picture Smart: Take photos of existing pollution.

- Body/Sport/Hand Smart: Organize teams to clean up the effects of pollution.
- Music Smart: Write a song about pollution.
- People Smart: Start an organization to put pressure on polluters.
- Self-Smart: Think of ways in which you can mediate pollution.

## DISCUSSION

1. Why is it important to know this information?

2. How does it change your ideas about intelligence?

3. How can you use it to help you do better in school?

4. How are your intelligence strengths related to possible occupations?

## OPTIONAL ACTIVTY

In small groups, have students tell of an experience in which they used their intelligence strengths and were successful. Students should get feedback from other students concerning their strengths.

# GARDNER'S SEVEN INTELLIGENCES

**WORD SMART** *(linguistic intelligence)*—the ability to use words and language, e.g., authors.

**NUMBER SMART** *(logical-mathematical intelligence)*—the ability to use numbers and logic and see relationships, e.g., scientists.

**PICTURE SMART** *(spatial intelligence)*—the ability to be sensitive to form, shape, color, and design, e.g., illustrators and photographers.

**BODY/SPORT/HAND SMART** *(bodily-kinesthetic intelligence)*—the ability to use one's whole body to express ideas and feelings, e.g., professional athletes and actors.

**MUSIC SMART** *(musical intelligence)*—the ability to enjoy rhythm and music and play instruments, e.g., rock stars, composers, and musicians.

**PEOPLE SMART** *(interpersonal intelligence)*—the ability to work successfully with people, e.g., politicians and salespeople.

**SELF-SMART** *(intrapersonal intelligence)*—the ability to work accurately by one's self and know one's strengths, e.g., entrepreneurs or "self-made" people.

*Source:* Armstrong, Thomas. 1994. *Multiple intelligences in the classroom.* Alexandria, VA: ASCD.

# SESSION 11:
# PUTTING IT ALL TOGETHER

## OVERVIEW
Students will take information that they have gathered about themselves in previous lessons and begin thinking about how these characteristics are related to career choice. This will prepare them to enter the next unit, which explores different occupations, with increased awareness of the kind of occupation that best suits them.

## DURATION
35 minutes

## OBJECTIVES
1. Students will be able to describe themselves accurately.

2. Students will understand how their interests, skills, and work values are important in considering occupational choice.

## MATERIALS NEEDED
student Life Clocks

Self-Knowledge activity sheet (copies for each student)

## PREPARATION
None

## ACTIVITY
1. Distribute copies of Self-Knowledge activity sheet and ask students to complete both sections.

## DISCUSSION
1. Once the class has completed the activity sheet, ask volunteers to share their analysis.

2. Review any issues that may arise.

# SELF-KNOWLEDGE

NAME: _____

DATE: _____

## EVALUATION

1. I have achieved the highest grades in high school in the following subjects:

2. My interest inventory revealed the following:

3. These are some skills I have developed that help me to be successful:

4. The 3 most important things that I want from a job are as follows:

5. Here are my intelligence strengths:

6. This data does or does not fit how I saw myself working at age 30:

7. Based on the above data, this is a possible career goal for me:

## ANALYSIS

1. Looking back at my Life Clock and the educational/training preparation I intend to pursue, is my career goal realistic?

2. Is it possible to change my preparation to meet my career goal?

3. Does my projected career goal fit into the way I saw myself organizing my time? Will it allow me the time to pursue leisure time activities that I enjoy?

4. Will my projected career goal allow me to do the things that I love to do?

# SESSION 12:

# INTERVIEWING

## OVERVIEW

Students will learn to articulate their interests, abilities, and work values by interviewing for their "dream job."

## DURATION

35 minutes

## OBJECTIVES

1. Students will be able to express themselves about their interests, abilities, and work values.
2. Students will be able to relate these characteristics to occupational choice.

## MATERIALS NEEDED

Dream Job Interviewer questionnaire (copies for each student)

## PREPARATION

None

## ACTIVITY

1. Divide the class into groups of 3. Student A will work with Student B to prepare him/her for the interview for the dream job. Student C will be the interviewer but will not be able to hear the preparation. Student C will only know what the projected job is and from that must prepare interview questions.

2. Distribute Dream Job Interviewer questionnaire and ask each student to fill in his/her dream job. Student B gives Student C the questionnaire so that he can develop interview questions while Students A and B prepare for the interview.

3. At the end of the interview, Student C will either hire the applicant (Student B), ask for more information, or reject the applicant, with explanation. Student A can help either the interviewer or the applicant by whispering helpful information to them.

4. Students switch roles until each has played each part.

## DISCUSSION
1. What did you learn from this activity?
2. What would you do differently next time?

## OPTIONAL ACTIVITY
Have retired adults come in and act as interviewers. Make the situation as realistic as possible. Have students practice with each other before being interviewed by an adult.

# DREAM JOB INTERVIEWER

**Dream job:** _____

**Interview questions:**

1. _____

   _____

2. _____

   _____

3. _____

   _____

4. _____

   _____

5. _____

   _____

6. _____

   _____

7. _____

   _____

8. _____

   _____

9. _____

   _____

10. _____

    _____

I would:

_____ hire the applicant
(Student B)

_____ask for more information

_____not hire the applicant

Why? _____

_____

_____

_____

# COMPETENCY CHECKLIST FOR UNIT ONE

As a result of my participation in Unit One, I . . .
*(Check those items of which you feel you have attained competency.)*

_____ know the difference between a job, an occupation, and a career.

_____ understand the process of career development.

_____ have considered my aspirations for the future.

_____ understand how I must prepare to attain my aspirations.

_____ appreciate the importance of work in my life.

_____ can relate my interests to career choice.

_____ have identified my preference for working with data, people, or things.

_____ can identify skills that I have developed.

_____ can relate my abilities to career decision-making.

_____ have identified my preferred work values.

_____ understand the importance of managing time.

_____ understand how gender bias can limit my choices.

_____ can name seven types of intelligence and know which are my strengths.

_____ understand the importance of interests, abilities, and work values in career decision-making.

_____ am able to tell others about my strengths, interests, and work values.

# • UNIT TWO: CAREER AND OCCUPATIONAL EXPLORATION
# Where Am I Going?

# UNIT TWO: CAREER AND OCCUPATIONAL EXPLORATION
# WHERE AM I GOING?

This unit gives students information about the labor market and the requirements to enter it. Through a series of activities, students will link occupational choice to lifestyle. In Sessions 13 and 14, they learn what it costs to maintain their "dream lifestyle" and then consider the jobs for which they would be eligible with their current skills and education. In most cases, they realize that they will have to have additional skills and education in order to obtain a job that would allow the lifestyle that they would like.

Session 15 introduces the concept of putting occupations with similar traits into clusters. Students become familiar with occupational clusters and use this information as a basis for further investigation of the labor market. They also learn that skills valued in one occupation can often be transferred to a similar occupation. In Session 16, students explore entry-level jobs in each of the clusters. They learn about the educational and other requirements needed for selected entry-level jobs. Session 17 deals with career ladders, the pathway to advancement in occupations.

Beginning with Session 18, students will be asked to perform certain activities outside the classroom. Students are asked to interview an employer to find out what attributes, other than technical skills and knowledge, employers desire in their employees. For example, employers will probably say that they want honest workers who come to work every day and on time. They might also say that they want team workers who get along well with others and who take pride in their work. Students will report on their findings and then, in class, rate themselves on the identified attributes by using their real jobs or chores outside of school.

Sessions 19 and 20 help to give students insight on the advantages and disadvantages of working for others as compared with self-employment. They are asked to compare these to their preferred work values identified in Unit One. For example, a student who preferred job security and low risk as work values would probably not be a good candidate for self-employment.

Session 21 helps students to appreciate the value of education and training as they consider worker know-how. Worker know-how is a list of 5 competency areas in which all workers must be proficient if they are to be successful in the 21st-century workplace. It is based on a 3-part foundation of basic skills, thinking skills, and personal qualities. Students should have insight into the fact that this foundation of basic skills has been forming over their lifetimes at school and at home and that the foundation must be strong if they are to attain the necessary competencies.

In Session 22, students interview adults about their work history—the jobs they have held, what they liked and disliked about them, what they would do differently. By learning from others, students will have insights into their own choices.

Session 23 gives students a look into their community—what opportunities are available and what is required to take advantage of them. This is a wonderful time for you to invite community business leaders into the classroom to talk about their work. You might also consider a career day in which as many community employers as possible come to your school to talk to students about their businesses. Usually a table for each employer is set up in a large area like a gymnasium. Students move from employer to employer in time slots of 15 to 20 minutes. Have students sign up for particular employers in advance so that the crowd is evenly distributed. If these activities are not possible, have students find an adult mentor in an occupation that interests them and either "shadow" the worker for a day or, at least, make contact to find out more specific information about the occupation and what it is like on a day-to-day basis.

The final session helps students to consider the global workplace. They are asked to identify trends—economic, political, environmental, and cultural—that might affect their local labor market. This helps students to understand the value of being informed and active citizens.

Unit One helped students to learn about themselves and how their interests, abilities, talents, and work values influence their lifework. Unit Two helps students to understand the labor market and the requirements to enter it. They are then ready for Unit Three—planning to get to where they want to be. Using their self-knowledge and labor market information, students will be ready to make tentative decisions about their future—knowing what they must do to achieve their goals.

# SESSION 13:
# THE COST OF LIVING

## OVERVIEW
Students will revisit their dream lifestyle from Unit One and research the cost of living for that lifestyle.

## DURATION
1 hour

## OBJECTIVES
1. Students will understand the cost of living of their preferred lifestyle.
2. Students will link lifestyle with occupational choice.
3. Students will understand that preparation must begin now if they are to attain their desired occupational goal.

## MATERIALS NEEDED
Dream Job Budget activity sheet (copies for each student)

sources of cost of living

## PREPARATION
Ask students to suggest resources for researching the cost of living.

## ACTIVITY
1. Ask students to revisit their dream occupation and lifestyle in Unit One.
2. Distribute Dream Job Budget activity sheet and ask students to calculate how much it costs to live in that style. Remind students that taxes and other fixed expenses must be deducted to find disposable income.
3. Have students research the monthly income of their dream job. Can they live the lifestyle they envisioned with that income? What occupations would support that kind of lifestyle?

## DISCUSSION

1. What are some math skills that you will need for budgeting?
2. What is the importance of budgeting?
3. What did you learn from this activity?
4. How does your occupation affect your lifestyle?
5. What does the government do with your taxes?

## OPTIONAL ACTIVITY

Have students take their budgets home and ask their parents if they are accurate in estimating the cost of living. Have students refigure their budgets after getting feedback from their parents.

# DREAM JOB BUDGET

## INSTRUCTIONS:

1. Fill in your monthly expenses on the budget sheet below.

2. Determine what gross monthly income you need to support your dream lifestyle.

| | | |
|---|---|---|
| **Gross monthly income** | | $ |
| Less payroll deductions (taxes, insurance, etc.) | | $ |
| **Net monthly income** | | $ |
| **Monthly expenses** | $ | |
| Housing | $ | |
| Food | $ | |
| Transportation (include maintenance of vehicle) | $ | |
| Clothing (include shoes, boots, clothing for all seasons and divide by 12) | $ | |
| Laundry/Cleaning Leisure Activities Utilities (electricity, etc.) | $ | |
| Other bills, expenses | $ | |
| Total expenses | $ | |
| **Net monthly income minus expenses** | | $ |
| Savings (gross income x .10) | | $ |

# SESSION 14:
# SCHOOL'S OUT!

## OVERVIEW
Students will research what jobs would be available to them if today were the last day of their formal education.

## DURATION
30–40 minutes

## OBJECTIVES
1. Students will have a better understanding of the value of their education.

2. Students will see how entry-level jobs are linked to education and training.

3. Students will consider the lifestyle that they could afford if they had to go to work tomorrow.

## MATERIALS NEEDED
completed Dream Job Budget activity sheets (from Session 13)

School's Out Budget activity sheet (copies for each student)

newspapers or other sources of available jobs

## PREPARATION
Bring any available information about local jobs to the classroom.

## ACTIVITY
1. Tell students that today will be their last day of school. There will not be any further education or training available. They must now be self-supporting and, due to unforeseen circumstances, will not be able to live at home.

2. Using newspapers and other sources of information, have students research the kinds of jobs for which they are qualified. Where could they get a job tomorrow? What job would it be? How much does it pay?

3. Using the estimated income from the job, have students fill out School's Out Budget activity sheet.

4. Ask students to compare the new budget with their Dream Job Budget.

# DISCUSSION

1. Were you surprised at the income of the job that you could qualify for tomorrow?

2. How does this affect your plans for continuing your education or training?

# OPTIONAL ACTIVITY

Have students fill out a job application for the job that they sought, and answer the following questions:

- What information do they need that they do not now have?
- Does the employer want employees with work experience?
- How can they get work experience while in school (volunteer jobs, part-time jobs, etc.)?

# SCHOOL'S OUT BUDGET

**Instrucions:**

1. Fill in your anticipated income and expenses.

2. Compare this budget with your Dream Job Budget.

| | | |
|---|---|---|
| **Gross monthly income** | | $ |
| Less payroll deductions (taxes, insurance, etc.) | | $ |
| **Net monthly income** | | $ |
| **Monthly expenses:** | $ | |
| Housing | $ | |
| Food | $ | |
| Transportation (include maintenance of vehicle) | $ | |
| Clothing (include shoes, boots, clothing for all seasons and divide by 12) | $ | |
| Laundry/Cleaning Leisure Activities Utilities (electricity, etc.) | $ | |
| Other bills, expenses | $ | |
| Total expenses | $ | |
| **Net monthly income minus expenses** | | $ |
| Savings | | $ |

# OCCUPATIONAL CLUSTERS

## OVERVIEW

Students will learn that occupations can be put into clusters according to the primary focus of the work. They will then review the occupations that they included on the Master List of Occupations, begun in Session 1, and group them into appropriate clusters.

## DURATION

30–40 minutes

## OBJECTIVES

1. Students will understand that most occupations share commonalities with other occupations.

2. Students will be able to group common occupations into clusters.

3. Students will see the value of grouping occupations.

## MATERIALS NEEDED

Occupational Clusters resource sheet (copies for each student)

Master List of Occupations (begun in Session 1)

or

Occupations resource sheet (copies for each student)

## PREPARATION

None

## ACTIVITY

1. Explain to the class that similar occupations can be grouped into clusters. There are many different types of clusters and it doesn't really matter which you use. For this session, use the list of occupational clusters below.

2. Using the Master List of Occupations or the Occupations resource sheet, try to put each occupation in the appropriate cluster.

3. Look at the occupations under each cluster. What characteristics do they have in common?

# DISCUSSION

1. What is the value of grouping occupations into clusters?
2. Can your interests be related to a specific occupational cluster?
3. Are your strengths compatible with occupations in that cluster?

# OCCUPATIONAL CLUSTERS

Agricultural & Manual Resources

Business & Office

Communication & Media

Construction

Consumer & Homemaking

Education

Fine Arts & Humanities

Manufacturing

Marine Science Environment

Marketing & Distribution

Personal/Public Service

Recreation & Hospitality

Transportation

# OCCUPATIONS

| | |
|---|---|
| accountant | garbage collector |
| ambulance driver | hotel clerk |
| attorney | insurance agent |
| beautician | lab technician |
| car salesperson | landscaper |
| carpenter | librarian |
| cartoonist | merchant mariner |
| cashier | nurse |
| computer programmer | painter |
| construction worker | police officer |
| doctor | soldier |
| electrician | teacher |
| factory worker | waitress |
| firefighter | |

# SESSION 16:
# ENTERING THE WORKPLACE

## OVERVIEW
Students will identify entry-level jobs in each cluster and will research the educational and training requirements for each job.

## DURATION
30–40 minutes

## OBJECTIVES
Students will gain an understanding of the educational and training requirements to enter the workplace in many different occupations.

## MATERIALS NEEDED
Occupational Clusters resource sheet [p. 95] (copies for each student)
Entry-Level Job Requirements: Examples (copies for each group)
Entry-Level Job Requirements activity sheet (6 copies for each group) (optional)

## PREPARATION
Be prepared to help students research the training and education required for entry-level jobs.

## ACTIVITY
1. Divide the class into small groups. Distribute Occupational Clusters resource sheet or write the occupational clusters from Session 15 on the board. Assign six clusters to each group. Have each group choose two occupations in each cluster.

2. Using available information, have students identify an entry-level job in each of the occupations.

3. Distribute Entry-Level Job Requirements: Examples and review. Have students determine entry-level requirements for each job that they have identified and summarize their findings on Entry-Level Job Requirements activity sheet.

4. Each group should report on findings. Remind each group to keep its work for the next session.

## DISCUSSION

1. What commonalities did you find in each cluster?

2. What do you think the pay would be for each of these jobs?

3. What do you think the demand is for each of these jobs?

## OPTIONAL ACTIVITY

Students could ask a local company for a list of its entry-level jobs, the requirements for the jobs, and the pay and benefits for the jobs.

# ENTRY-LEVEL JOB REQUIREMENTS

---

**CLUSTER:** Transportation

**OCCUPATION:** Truck driver

**JOB:** Driving a van for a furniture company

**ENTRY-LEVEL REQUIREMENTS:**

- Must be at least 21 years old.

- Must have a Class 1 driver's license.

- Must have certificate of competence from accredited truck-driving school.

- Must have a good driving record. Must be able to lift heavy loads.

---

**CLUSTER:** Recreation and Hospitality

**OCCUPATION:** Hotel worker

**JOB:** Clerk at Central Hotel

**ENTRY-LEVEL REQUIREMENTS:**

- Must have good interpersonal skills.

- Must have a solid background in math.

- Must be computer proficient.

- Must have completed hotel orientation course.

- Must be able to work irregular hours.

---

# ENTRY-LEVEL JOB REQUIREMENTS

Using Occupational Clusters, identify 2 entry-level jobs in each of the occupational clusters assigned and determine the requirements for each job.

**CLUSTER:**

**OCCUPATION:**

**JOB:**

**ENTRY-LEVEL REQUIREMENTS:**

1.

2.

3.

4.

5.

**CLUSTER:**

**OCCUPATION:**

**JOB:**

**ENTRY-LEVEL REQUIREMENTS:**

1.

2.

3.

4.

5.

# SESSION 17:
# CAREER LADDERS

## OVERVIEW

Most people expect to advance in their chosen occupation. The usual progression of jobs in a particular occupation is called a career ladder. Students will take the entry-level jobs that they have identified and describe the series of future jobs advancing in that occupation that could be available with appropriate training and good performance.

## DURATION

30–40 minutes

## OBJECTIVES

1. Students will understand the concept of career ladders.

2. Students will recognize that advancement in an occupation is dependent on good job performance and appropriate training.

3. Students will realize that advancement is dependent on continued education and learning of new skills.

## MATERIALS NEEDED

student Life Clocks
completed Entry-Level Job Requirements activity sheets from Session 16
Career Ladder activity sheet (copies for each group) (optional)

## PREPARATION

Remind students to bring their Life Clocks and the completed Entry-Level Job Requirements activity sheets from Session 16.

## ACTIVITY

1. Refer students back to the Life Clock that they created. How many years do they believe they will be in the workplace?

2. Ask students if they want to work at the entry-level job that whole time. In some cases, the job does not change. For example, science teachers may remain science teachers for 30 years because that is their chosen profession. However, they might become head of the department or an administrator in the system. Conversely, a dishwasher in a restaurant would probably look forward to advancement.

3. Reassemble the groups from Session 16 and tell them to use their completed Entry-Level Job Requirements activity sheets to devise possible career ladders of advancement for the entry-level jobs that they analyzed.

EXAMPLES:

Store clerk

- Department assistant manager
- Department manager
- Assistant buyer
- Buyer
- Store Manager

Dishwasher

- Busboy
- Waiter
- Maitre'd
- Assistant manager
- Manager

4. What additional training or education is needed to progress to each of the levels?

# DISCUSSION

1. Were you surprised at the number of steps one must take to advance?

2. What do you think is the difference in pay between the entry-level job and the top job in that occupation?

3. What would the career ladder of your dream occupation look like?

4. How long do you think it would take you to advance to each level?

# OPTIONAL ACTIVITY

Have someone from a local company or business talk to the students about advancement from entry-level jobs. Be sure they point out additional education or training that would be needed to progress up the career ladder.

# HOMEWORK ASSIGNMENT

Give students the following assignment to complete outside of class before the next session:

Each student is to interview an employer about work attributes, other than the specific skills and knowledge needed for the job, that the employer wants in an employee. If an employer is not available, students can interview any adult about attributes that they think are important in the workplace.

# CAREER LADDER

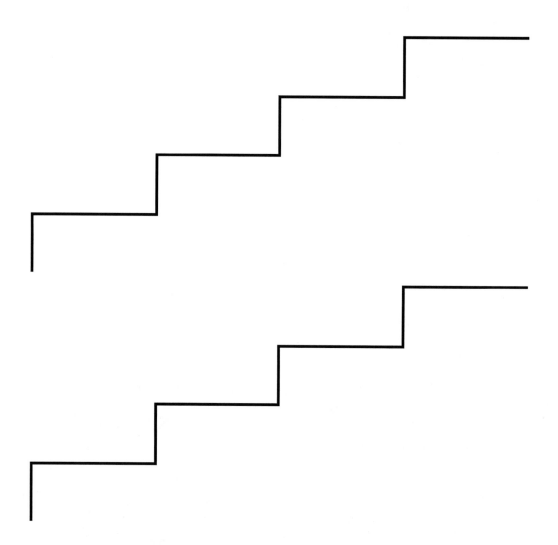

# POSITIVE WORK ATTRIBUTES

## OVERVIEW
Students will learn first hand, by interviewing employers in the community, what attributes employers want prospective workers to have.

## DURATION
Interviews are done outside of class. Reporting of results: 30 minutes

## OBJECTIVES
1. Students will gain first-hand knowledge of the kinds of attitudes that are conducive to success at work.

2. Students will be able to assess their attitudes about work.

## MATERIALS NEEDED
Attribute activity sheet (copies for all students)

## PREPARATION
Make sure that students have completed their homework from the previous session: interview an employer or adult about work attributes desired in an employee.

## ACTIVITY
1. Ask students to form small groups and share their lists of worker attributes, including the source of their information.

2. Ask each group to compile a master list of attributes.

3. Ask one group to put its list on the board. Then invite a second group to add any additional attributes to the list. Continue until every group has had a chance to add to the list. Combine similar attributes. Explain that if two applicants have equal skills, these attributes may make the difference in getting a job.

4. The attributes that are important in the workplace are usually formed over a lifetime. Distribute Attribute activity sheet and discuss. Ask students to complete the sheet.

# DISCUSSION

1. What did you learn from the list of desired attributes?

2. Are there areas in which you need improvement?

3. Would your lack of these attributes be tolerated in the workplace? Examples would be forgetting or not being on time.

4. What can you do to improve?

# OPTIONAL ACTIVITY

Have students interview each other as if they were applying for a job. The employer should ask applicants to give examples of how they demonstrate in their lives that they are dependable, on time, responsible, take pride in work, etc. (Use the list of attributes from the board.)

# ATTRIBUTE

## Instructions:

1. List chores or jobs for which you are currently responsible in the "jobs" column of the table below.

2. In the "attributes" column, list the attributes that are important in that task.

3. In the "performance" column, assess how well you perform the task in relation to the attributes. The following is an example:

| JOBS | ATTRIBUTES | PERFORMANCE |
|---|---|---|
| 1. Feeding the dog | • Being on time<br>• Being dependable<br>• Caring | • Sometimes forget<br>• Am often late<br>• Do care about my dog |

| JOBS | ATTRIBUTES | PERFORMANCE |
|---|---|---|
| 1. | | |
| 2. | | |
| 3. | | |
| 4. | | |
| 5. | | |
| 6. | | |

# SESSION 19:

# WORKING FOR OTHERS

## OVERVIEW
Students will think about the employer-employee relationship and the pros and cons of working for someone.

## DURATION
20–30 minutes

## OBJECTIVES
Students will think about the advantages and disadvantages of working for someone else.

## MATERIALS NEEDED
completed Work Values activity sheets (from Session 7)

Working for Others evaluation sheet (copies for each student)

## PREPARATION
None

## ACTIVITY
1. There are basically 2 types of employment: working for others and working for one's self.

2. Distribute and review Working for Others evaluation sheets. Ask students to complete the sheet.

3. Write "Working for Others" on the board and make 2 columns under the title. Label one "pro" and the other "con."

4. Compile a master list of "pros" and "cons" from the evaluation sheets and discuss.

## DISCUSSION

1. When you dreamed about your ideal job, did someone else employ you?

2. At this point, do you see yourself working for someone else or creating your own job?

3. How might your attitude change if you had a family to support?

## OPTIONAL ACTIVITY

Contact the personnel department of a local company and find out what kinds of benefits are offered to employees. Also find out about working hours and responsibilities of workers.

# Evaluation Sheet
# Working for Others

## Instructions:

1. List positive reasons to work for someone else in the "pro" column of the table below. Examples are security, paid holidays and vacations, sick leave, don't have to worry about financial condition of company, etc.

2. List the disadvantages under the "con" column. Examples are loss of control over work, advancement is up to employer, work for prescribed pay with little opportunity for reward for performance, etc.

3. Compare the "pros" and "cons" against your preferred work values (analyzed in your Work Values activity sheet).

| WORKING FOR OTHERS | |
|---|---|
| **Pro** | **Con** |
| 1. | |
| 2. | |
| 3. | |
| 4. | |
| 5. | |
| 6. | |
| 7. | |
| 8. | |
| 9. | |
| 10. | |

# SESSION 20:
# SELF-EMPLOYMENT

## OVERVIEW
Students will consider the advantages and disadvantages of self-employment.

## DURATION
30 minutes

## OBJECTIVES
1. Students will understand that self-employment is a viable alternative.

2. Students will identify the risks of becoming self-employed.

3. Students will identify the advantages of self-employment.

## MATERIALS NEEDED
completed Work Values activity sheets (from Session 7)

Self-Employment evaluation sheet (copies for each student)

## PREPARATION
None

## ACTIVITY
1. Distribute and review Self-Employment evaluation sheets. Ask students to complete the sheets.

2. Write "Self-Employed" on the board and make two columns under the title. Label one "pro" and the other "con."

3. Compile a master list of "pros" and "cons" from the evaluation sheets and discuss.

## DISCUSSION
1. When you dreamed about your ideal job, were you self-employed?

2. Considering the trends and demographics of your location, what business could you start?

3. Would you be offering a product or service?

4. How would you assess the competition?

5. Where would you get the financial resources to start a business?

 ## OPTIONAL ACTIVITY
Invite a self-employed person to your class to tell about how he/she got started and what he/she would list as pros and cons.

# EVALUATION SHEET
# SELF-EMPLOYMENT

## Instructions:

1. List positive reasons to be self-employed in the "pro" column of the table below.

4. List the disadvantages under the "con" column.

5. Compare the "pros" and "cons" against your preferred work values (analyzed in your Work Values activity sheet).

| SELF-EMPLOYMENT | |
|---|---|
| Pro | Con |
| 1. | |
| 2. | |
| 3. | |
| 4. | |
| 5. | |
| 6. | |
| 7. | |
| 8. | |
| 9. | |
| 10. | |

# SESSION 21:
# WORKER KNOW-HOW

## OVERVIEW
Students will learn about the competencies that all workers will need to be successful in the 21st century.

## DURATION
30 minutes

## OBJECTIVES
1. Students will understand basic competencies that are needed to be successful in the workplace.
2. Students will see the relationship between their education and their success in the workplace.

## MATERIALS NEEDED
Five Competencies resource sheet (copies for each student)

First Job activity sheet (copies for each student)

## PREPARATION
None

## ACTIVITY
1. Distribute and review Five Competencies recourse sheet.
2. In small groups, have students choose an occupation and identify ways that the five competencies might be used.

   For example, here is how beauticians might use the five competencies:

   **RESOURCES:** have to plan the most effective use of facilities, and manage time and money wisely.

   **INTERPERSONAL:** must serve customers in a pleasant manner and listen carefully.

   **INFORMATION:** should acquire the latest information on personal products and may use a computer to keep inventory straight.

**Systems:** must understand how marketing, service, and purchase of materials are all interrelated.

**Technology:** use the latest technology to offer the best service for the least cost.

3. Have small groups report on findings.

## DISCUSSION

1. Where does one obtain the foundation on which the competencies are built?

2. How can these competencies be attained?

## OPTIONAL ACTIVITY

Have students interview workers to find out how they use the competencies. They should also ask how important the foundation elements are to their success.

## HOMEWORK ASSIGNMENT

Before the next session, have students interview a parent or other adult about their work history, using the First Job activity sheet.

# RESOURCE SHEET
# FIVE COMPETENCIES

A few years ago, a group of educators and business leaders came together to identify universal skills needed for employment. They knew that good jobs will increasingly require people who can put knowledge to work. They called the skills needed for effective job performance "Workplace Know-How." This know-how has two elements: competencies and a foundation.

The five **competencies** are as follows:

- **Resources**: Identifies, organizes, plans, and allocates resources (time, money, material and facilities, human resources)

- **Interpersonal**: Works with others (team member, teaches others, serves clients, exercises leadership, negotiates, works with diversity)

- **Information**: Acquires and uses information (acquires, evaluates, organizes, maintains, interprets, and communicates information); uses computers to process information

- **Systems**: Understands complex inter-relationships (understands social, organizational, and technological systems, monitors and corrects performance, improves or designs systems)

- **Technology**: Works with a variety of technologies (selects technology, applies technology to task, maintains and troubleshoots equipment)

The competencies differ from a person's technical knowledge. For example, both accountants and engineers manage resources, information systems, and technology but in different contexts.

These competencies are based on a three-part **foundation**. The elements of the foundation are the following:

- **Basic skills** (reading, writing, mathematics and computational skills, listening, and speaking)

- **Thinking skills** (creative thinking, decision-making, problem-solving, visualizing, knowing how to learn, and reasoning)

- **Personal qualities** (responsibility, self-esteem, sociability, self-management, and integrity/honesty)

# FIRST JOB

**Name of adult:** _____

**Job:**_____

1. How did they obtain this job? (first job)

2. What skills did they use?

3. How were they prepared to do this job?

4. What did they like about the job? Why?

5. What did they dislike about the job? Why?

6. Why did they change jobs?


**Next job:**

Repeat same questions until current job. On current job, change question 6 to "Would they like to change jobs?"

# SESSION 22:
# LEARNING FROM OTHERS

## OVERVIEW

Through interviews, students will learn about work history and how interests and abilities influence choices.

## DURATION

30–40 minutes

## OBJECTIVES

1. Students will have an understanding of various work roles.

2. Students will learn how choices were made that led to job changes.

## MATERIALS NEEDED

Completed First Job activity sheets from Session 21

Learning from Others activity sheet (copies for each student)

## PREPARATION

Make sure that students have completed the homework assignment given at the end of previous session: interview a parent or other adult about their work history.

## ACTIVITY

1. Have students report on their interviews.

2. Ask students to complete Learning from Others activity sheet and attach it to their completed First Job activity sheet to be put in their portfolio.

## OPTIONAL ACTIVITY

Interview grandparents, uncles, aunts, siblings, etc., using the same format, and design a family work tree.

# LEARNING FROM OTHERS

**Instructions:**

Review your findings from your First Job activity sheet and answer the following questions:

1. What surprised you about your findings?

2. Do you think the adults might have done things differently knowing what they do now?

3. What insights do you have about your choices?

# SESSION 23:
# COMMUNITY INVOLVEMENT

## OVERVIEW
Students will have a better understanding of the opportunities available in their community by visiting a local business or job service office.

## DURATION
Depends on activity

## OBJECTIVES
Students will have a better understanding of the local job market.

## MATERIALS NEEDED
None

## PREPARATION
Ask someone who deals with job placement to visit the class. Or if you have a large industry or business in your community, contact the human resources (personnel) office to see if you could bring your class to its site to explore various jobs performed in the company.

  ## ACTIVITY

1. Tell students that someone who deals with job placement will be visiting the class, or that they will be visiting a business.
2. Ask the class to prepare an interview format to find out the following:
   - What are all the jobs available in that company (from janitor to president)?
   - How are hiring decisions made? Are they made by each department or by a central department?
   - What basic skills and/or credentials are needed?
   - What advice would they give students concerning preparation for the workplace?
3. Add other questions generated by the students.
4. Conduct the interview.

# DISCUSSION

1. Name three things you learned about the labor market.

2. What surprised you?

3. How can you use this information for your own preparation?


# OPTIONAL ACTIVITY

If a group visit is not possible, have individual students contact workers in jobs that interest them. Discuss the possibility of a mentoring relationship.

SESSION 24:
# THE GLOBAL COMMUNITY

## OVERVIEW
Students will study factors outside their immediate community that might influence the local labor market.

## DURATION
30–40 minutes

## OBJECTIVES
1. Students will understand that influences outside their community can affect the local labor market.
2. Students will appreciate the importance of following the news to identify trends that might affect them.

## MATERIALS NEEDED
Five Guiding Principles resource sheet (page 37)
Trends activity sheet (copies for each student)
newspapers, magazines, reports of TV shows

## PREPARATION
Have students bring in magazines, etc. that might provide national and world news.

## ACTIVITY
1. Organize the students into small groups. Ask each group to use the resources available to compile a list of trends that might influence the job market in their town. These trends might be political (national and world), economic, cultural, or environmental.
2. Compile a master list of trends and write them on the board. Ask students how each trend might affect the local job market.

## DISCUSSION

1. Review Five Guiding Principles of career-building. How can global influences make a difference in your choices?

2. How can you use knowledge about the trends to your advantage?

## OPTIONAL ACTIVITY

Have each student identify a trend and write a possible scenario about its effect on local employment.

# TRENDS

Trends that may influence the job market in my town are the following:

| Political |
|---|
| National |
| |
| World |
| |

| Economic |
|---|
| |

| Cultural |
|---|
| |

| Environmental |
|---|
| |

| Other |
|---|
| |

# COMPETENCY CHECKLIST FOR UNIT TWO

As a result of my participation in Unit Two, I . . .
*(Check those items of which you feel you have attained competency.)*

_____  understand the relationship of income to lifestyle.

_____  know that preparation must begin now if I am to attain my desired lifestyle.

_____  understand the connection between education/training and entry-level jobs.

_____  can explain the concept of occupational clusters.

_____  can name at least 4 occupational clusters.

_____  know requirements for entry into the workplace in several occupations.

_____  can explain the concept of career ladders.

_____  understand that advancement depends on continued learning and training.

_____  can name 4 positive work attributes that employers desire.

_____  can identify attributes that I must improve.

_____  can cite the advantages and disadvantages of working for others.

_____  can cite the advantages and disadvantages of self-employment.

_____  understand the concept of worker know-how.

_____  can identify the 5 competency areas of worker know-how.

_____  understand the various work roles that people experience.

_____  have an understanding of the local labor market.

_____  appreciate how global influences can affect the local labor market.

# • UNIT THREE: CAREER PLANNING
## How Do I Get There?

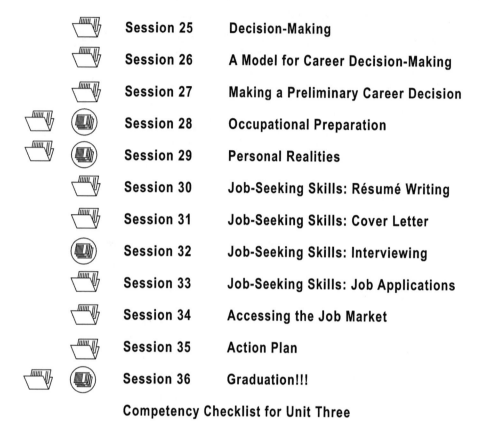

# UNIT THREE: CAREER PLANNING
# HOW DO I GET THERE?

This final unit takes the students through the decision-making process to the actual skills needed in seeking employment. Session 25 stimulates their thinking about the decision-making process. Session 26 introduces a model for career decision-making and gives students practice in using it. In Session 27, they are asked to make a preliminary career choice using the decision-making model.

Students research the requirements for entering their selected occupations in Session 28. They are then asked to consider the personal realities of their lives in Session 29, which discusses the challenges of change and explores potential barriers to attaining their occupational goals. Through shared problem-solving, students learn to consider many alternatives.

The next part of Unit Three is concerned with job-seeking skills. Session 30 introduces writing résumés and gives students opportunities to construct their own. Session 31 follows with practice in writing cover letters to accompany the résumés. In Session 32, students learn about job interviews and practice them through role-playing situations. Job applications are the topic of Session 33. Finally, students think about how they can access the labor market in Session 34. Traditional ways of finding a job are discussed, but the emphasis is on "networking"—the method through which most people actually find jobs.

In Session 35, students are asked to make a commitment to action. By now, they should have a career goal in mind and know what they must do to reach that goal. Sometimes it is helpful to "plan backwards." Starting with their goal, they can plan backwards to where they are now—what courses they must take, what experiences they should have, whom they should contact to learn more about the occupation, etc. Students are asked to share their action plans with another person. This person should be someone who can and will be supportive of the student's achieving the goal. This person is also their "conscience"— someone who will ask about progress toward the goal—and a reminder of the commitment to action.

The last session is an opportunity for students to discuss *Focus on the Future* and to give feedback on their experiences. If the students took the pre-test at the first session, you may want to give it again as a post-test. Students should be able to see their growth in the career development process. Finally, having a "graduation" ceremony brings closure to the program. You might give a certificate of completion to each student.

*Focus on the Future* has taken students through self-assessment, occupational exploration, and, finally, decision-making and action. Students may change their minds about their career goals, but the process they have learned will continue to help them throughout their lives. Congratulations to you for helping your students answer the questions: Who Am I? Where Am I Going? and How Do I Get There? You have made a difference in their lives.

# SESSION 25:
# DECISION-MAKING

## OVERVIEW
Students will consider how they make decisions in their lives and analyze the process they use.

## DURATION
30 minutes

## OBJECTIVES
1. Students will understand that decision-making is a process.

2. Students will be able to analyze how they make decisions.

## MATERIALS NEEDED
Monarch, Majority, and Mayhem activity sheet (copies for each student) (optional)

## PREPARATION
None

## ACTIVITY
1. Ask students to think about all the decisions they have made that day. The first decision may have been to get up in the morning. Others may have been concerned with what to wear, whom to call, what to say, etc. We make decisions all day long without much thought as to the process of how we decide. Most decisions are based on previous experience. Sometimes we ask for advice from others; sometimes we weigh the pros and cons; and sometimes we decide because it "feels right." When we need to make important decisions, we must have a process to consider all perspectives.

2. Have students write, draw a diagram, or make a model of how they make decisions.

3. Have each student share his or her method with another student.

4. Ask for volunteers to tell how they make decisions. Make a list of the different ways that people make decisions.

## DISCUSSION

1. Does your method of deciding change according to the decision to be made?

2. Were you surprised that others make decisions differently?

3. Who do you go to when you have an important decision to make?

4. What do you think your decisions are ultimately based upon?


## OPTIONAL ACTIVITY

1. Distribute Monarch, Majority, and Mayhem activity sheet and review.

2. Ask the students as a class to define the terms monarch, majority, and mayhem and write the definition on their activity sheets.

3. Divide the class into small groups and have students make a group decision on their favorite color (or dessert, animal, song, etc.) using the three methods. Give 3–5 minutes for each method.

4. Ask the students to complete Part 2 of the activity sheet.

ACTIVITY SHEET
# MONARCH, MAJORITY, AND MAYHEM

## PART 1
Define:

1. Monarch:

2. Majority:

3. Mayhem:

## PART 2
After you have completed the group activity, answer the following questions.

1. How time efficient was each method?

2. How involved were the group members?

3. How did group members react to each decision?

4. Were group members satisfied with each decision?

5. Which method do you personally prefer?

SESSION 26:

# A MODEL FOR CAREER DECISION-MAKING

## OVERVIEW
Students will become familiar with a model for career decision-making and practice using the model.

## DURATION
30–45 minutes

## OBJECTIVES
1. Students will understand and use a decision-making process.

2. Students will understand the skills needed to make career decisions.

## MATERIALS NEEDED
Decision-Making Chart (copies for each student)

Career Decision-Making Model (copies for each student)

## PREPARATION
None

## ACTIVITY
1. Distribute Decision-Making Chart and discuss the decision-making process.

2. Form the class into small groups. Distribute copies of Career Decision-Making Model and review.

3. Instruct each group to choose a fictitious person and occupation and complete the model.

4. Once the groups have completed their models, discuss them with the entire class.

5. Remind students that this was a make-believe situation. In the next session, they complete the model for themselves.

## DISCUSSION
1. What was the most difficult part of this process?

2. Do you think it will be easier or more difficult to decide for yourself? Why or why not?

# DECISION-MAKING CHART

Decide to decide

Gather information about yourself

Explore the labor market

Generate options and consequences

Make a decision

Put a plan together

Act

Evaluate your progress and modify

# CAREER DECISION-MAKING MODEL

NAME: _____

1. **DECIDE TO DECIDE:** You are ready to make a decision about your future. Remember that decisions can be changed and may change as you grow and mature.

   • The decision I'm ready to make is this (to choose an occupation to prepare for):

   • Here is the time when I want this to happen:

2. **GATHER INFORMATION ABOUT YOURSELF:** In Unit One you gathered information about your lifestyle, interest, abilities, strengths, and work values.

   • My 3 highest areas of interest are the following:

   • I prefer to work with (people, data/ideas, or things):

   • I have developed the following skills:

   • My 3 most important work values are as follows:

   • My strengths are in the following types of intelligence:

**3. EXPLORE THE LABOR MARKET**: In Unit Two you learned about the world of work and considered national and global trends that might affect your entry into the labor market.

- Career options that interest me are these (list 3):

**4. GENERATE OPTIONS AND CONSEQUENCES**: Consider each career option from the perspective of your interest, abilities, intelligence strengths, and work values.

- Place 3 career options in the "Title" boxes. Rank each career option according to how well each provides opportunities for job satisfaction.

| TITLE | OPTION #1 | OPTION #2 | OPTION #3 |
|---|---|---|---|
| Interests | | | |
| Category preference (data/people/things) | | | |
| Abilities/Skills | | | |
| Intelligence strengths | | | |
| Work values | | | |

4—very satisfying  3—fair   2—tolerable  1—no way

**5. MAKE A DECISION**: Which option do you wish to pursue?

- Having given considerable thought to this decision, I am interested in pursuing the following occupational choice:

**6. PUT TOGETHER A PLAN**: What are the basic steps to prepare for that option?

- I have worked out a plan for how I will prepare for my future. The basic steps are the following:

  1.

  2.

  3.

  4.
  (Add as many steps as needed.)

7. **ACT**: What training will you need to pursue your goal?

- In order to pursue my career option, I will obtain the following training/education:

- To obtain the training/education I need to be successful in my chosen occupation, I will do the following:

8. **EVALUATE YOUR PROGRESS AND MODIFY**: You will change and so may your career goal.

- I will look at this plan again in (days, months, years) and evaluate and modify as necessary.

# SESSION 27:
# MAKING A PRELIMINARY CAREER DECISION

## OVERVIEW
Students will make a preliminary decision about their career choice using the career decision-making model.

## DURATION
30–45 minutes

## OBJECTIVES
1. Students will understand and use a decision-making process.

2. Students will understand how change and growth affect decisions.

3. Students will have skills to make career decisions.

## MATERIALS NEEDED
Decision-Making Chart (page 138) (copies for each student)

Career Decision-Making Model (page 139) (copies for each student)

## PREPARATION
None

## ACTIVITY
1. Distribute copies of Decision-Making Chart and review the process.

2. Review the key points of Session 26. Distribute copies of Career Decision-Making Model to students and ask them to complete the form for themselves.

## DISCUSSION
1. Was it difficult to make a preliminary career decision? Why or why not?

2. What are the barriers to pursuing your career choice?

3. Who or what can help you to pursue your career choice?

# SESSION 28:

# OCCUPATIONAL PREPARATION

## OVERVIEW
Students will research the requirements of entry into the occupation that they have selected. They will also consider alternative methods of obtaining the necessary skills and knowledge needed.

## DURATION
30 minutes

## OBJECTIVES
1. Students will understand the requirements to enter their chosen occupation.

2. Students will learn about alternative ways to obtain the necessary skills and knowledge needed.

## MATERIALS NEEDED
Occupational Preparation activity sheet (copies for each student)

## PREPARATION
None

## ACTIVITY
1. Distribute Occupational Preparation activity sheet and review. Have students research the entry requirements for their chosen occupation. Information may be available in reference books in the library; from government publications; from trade unions or professional associations; or from talking to someone in that occupation. Tell students to list all of the requirements they can find on the activity sheet.

2. Ask students to consider the entry requirements and how they will be able to attain them. The traditional training and preparation may be through secondary vocational courses, post-secondary vocational training, university programs, or apprenticeships. Ask students to list on the activity sheet the formal ways by which they intend to train for their occupation.

3. Have students list other ways to attain the entry requirements for their selected occupation. These might include reading journals or books to obtain knowledge, going to special workshops, joining the military service, getting on-the-job training, volunteering to help someone in that occupation, and/or taking a temporary job that would add to their skills.

## DISCUSSION

1. Did you discover more than one way to get the necessary preparation to enter your selected occupation?

2. Are you still interested in pursuing that occupation or would you like to reconsider your preliminary decision?

## OPTIONAL ACTIVITY

Have students talk to a worker practicing their selected occupation about the preparation necessary to enter the field and ask the worker for any words of wisdom that he/she might impart for someone just beginning.

# OCCUPATIONAL PREPARATION

## OCCUPATION:

### ENTRY REQUIREMENTS:

1.

2.

3.

4.

5.

### FORMAL WAYS TO OBTAIN TRAINING

1.

2.

3.

4.

5.

### OTHER WAYS TO OBTAIN TRAINING

1.

2.

3.

4.

5.

# SESSION 29:

# PERSONAL REALITIES

## OVERVIEW

Students will think about their unique lives in relation to the preliminary decisions that they have made. As they look at the realities of their lives, they consider ways to overcome possible barriers to pursuing their goals.

## DURATION

30 minutes

## OBJECTIVES

1. Students will be able to look objectively at their circumstances.

2. Students will understand that they can overcome barriers to their goals.

3. Students will be able to list sources of support.

4. Students will appreciate the importance of planning for their futures.

## MATERIALS NEEDED

Personal Realities activity sheet (copies for each student)

## PREPARATION

None

  ## ACTIVITY

1. Tell students the following:

> Leaving the educational world in which you have lived for several years and going into the workplace constitute a major change in your life. For many people, change is a challenge. It means letting go of the known and familiar and moving toward the unknown and unfamiliar. Today you will look at the changes that you have already experienced and how you met the challenges of those changes. Then each of you will have an opportunity to think about the uniqueness of your life situation and the changes and challenges that may emerge as you prepare to enter the world of work.

2. Distribute Personal Realities activity sheet and direct the class in completing the form. Ask students to list 3 changes that they have made in the last 5 years. Tell them to think about these changes as they answer the questions in Part 2: How I React to Change.

3. Ask students to think about their preliminary occupational goal and answer the following question:

    Are there barriers to my obtaining the necessary training/education needed to pursue my occupational goal (financial, family responsibilities, transportation, eligibility to get into preparatory program, etc.)?

4. Have students list each barrier on the activity sheet and think about possible solutions. Urge them to consider friends and family that might support them, government agencies that offer help, and/or teachers or advisers who may know of available resources.

5. Ask students to list at least one step toward a solution for each barrier.

6. Divide the class into pairs and have each pair discuss their situations and come up with even more alternatives.

7. Tell students to talk to their parents about their concerns and possible steps to overcome barriers.

## DISCUSSION

1. What did you learn from this exercise?

2. Do you now feel that it is possible to pursue your preliminary occupational goal? Why or why not?

3. What help do you need now?

# PERSONAL REALITIES

**PART 1:** The 3 Changes I Have Made

The 3 changes I have made in the last 5 years are the following:

1.

2.

3.

**PART 2:** How I React to Change

Answer the following questions:

a. When I have had to change, the following things bothered me the most:

b. These things have gotten in my way as I grew and changed:

c. These things have excited me about change:

d. These are ways I have found to help me manage change:

**PART 3:** Barriers to Achieving My Preliminary Occupational Goal

List the barriers to your goal and write down any possible solutions.

| BARRIERS | SOLUTIONS |
| --- | --- |
| | |
| | |
| | |
| | |
| | |

SESSION 30:

# JOB-SEEKING SKILLS: RÉSUMÉ WRITING

## OVERVIEW

Students will learn about the contents of a résumé and will construct their own.

## DURATION

45 minutes

## OBJECTIVES

1. Students will understand the concept of a résumé.

2. Students will be able to construct their own résumé.

## MATERIALS NEEDED

Résumé resource sheet (copies for each student)

## PREPARATION

None

## ACTIVITY

1. Distribute Résumé resource sheet and review each section carefully with the class.

2. Have students construct their own résumés as if they were applying for their ideal job.

3. In small groups, have students critique each other's résumé.

4. Collect the résumés and make suggestions for improvement. Return the résumés to students.

5. Explain that a cover letter usually accompanies a résumé. Tell students that they will learn how to write an effective cover letter in the next session.

## DISCUSSION

1. What was the most difficult part of writing your résumé?

2. What help do you need to construct your next résumé?

# OPTIONAL ACTIVITY

Have students choose a job from the classified ads and write a résumé in response to it.

When people are ready to apply for jobs, they must be able to convince others that they are qualified and should be hired. One tool to accomplish this is called the résumé. The résumé is a listing of a person's accomplishments and work/education history. It is usually the first impression that an employer has of an applicant. Therefore, it is very important that a résumé show the applicant's best features.

Employers usually receive many résumés and may give only minimum attention to them. Therefore, if the résumé catches their eye, the applicant will have a better chance of getting an interview. Think of the résumé as an advertisement to get you an interview. There are many formats for a résumé. Here is an outline that reflects the latest thinking.

## COMPONENTS OF A RÉSUMÉ

- Contact Information
- Job Objective
- Major Relevant Accomplishments
- Work Experience
- Education and Training
- Personal Information

**CONTACT INFORMATION:** At the very top of the résumé, put your contact information: name, address, phone number and email address.

**JOB OBJECTIVE:** This is the place to put your job objective. It should match the description of the job being applied for. Here is an example: "Job Objective: I am seeking a position as an electrician with a construction company."

**MAJOR RELEVANT ACCOMPLISHMENTS:** Employers want more than a list of job duties or where you worked and when. They are interested in how well you have done your job, what skills and experience you have to offer, what your strengths are, and what you have accomplished. The following is an example:

Completed vocational course in commercial electricity with top grade in class.

Was runner-up in the city vocational school contest, electricity category.

Worked as apprentice electrician with Morgan Electric Company. In this capacity I wired the Smith Office Complex under the direction of Mr. James Morgan. He is available as a reference.

Received basic commercial electricity license in May 2005.

**WORK EXPERIENCE:** You can put other jobs held or tasks done that demonstrate your personal or occupational competence. Refer back to Unit One: Session 6: Skills Inventory.

**EDUCATION AND TRAINING:** List any courses taken or certificates received that are relevant to your job application.

**PERSONAL INFORMATION:** This may be added but is not necessary in a résumé.

# SESSION 31:
# JOB-SEEKING SKILLS: COVER LETTER

## OVERVIEW
Students will learn about the essential components of a cover letter and will write one to go with their résumé.

## DURATION
30 minutes

## OBJECTIVES
1. Students will learn about the components of a cover letter.

2. Students will practice writing a cover letter.

## MATERIALS NEEDED
Cover Letter Basics (copies for each student)

## PREPARATION
None

 ## ACTIVITY
1. Distribute copies of Cover Letter Basics and review carefully.

2. Tell students to write a cover letter to accompany the résumé for seeking their selected job.

3. Collect the cover letters and make suggestions for improvement. Return the letters to students.

## DISCUSSION
1. What was the most difficult part of writing a cover letter?

2. What additional information or assistance would have helped? Where could you have gotten this information or assistance?

# COVER LETTER BASICS

Cover letters used to simply tell the employer where the applicant heard about the job and stated that a résumé was attached. Today's cover letter is used to provide additional information and to interest the employer in granting an interview.

The cover letter should include the following:

- the name of a person known to both the applicant and the employer, if possible
- why the applicant would like to have the job
- the applicant's knowledge of the organization (business, institution, etc.)
- additional information not included in the résumé
- mention of the skills, background, and strengths that match the job requirements
- any special circumstances that should be known
- a petition for an interview or other follow-up

The cover letter should be short and easy to read. Avoid long paragraphs and keep the lists short.

# SESSION 32:
# JOB-SEEKING SKILLS: INTERVIEWING

## OVERVIEW

Students will learn about job interviews and will role-play an interview both as an employer and an applicant.

## DURATION

30 minutes

## OBJECTIVES

1. Students will learn effective interviewing techniques.

2. Through practice, students will feel comfortable with an interview.

## MATERIALS NEEDED

Interview resource sheet

## PREPARATION

None

## ACTIVITY

1. Distribute Interview resource sheet and review in detail with the class.

2. In groups of 3, have students role-play an interview for the job that is the target of the résumé and cover letter. They should take turns being the employer, the job applicant, and the observer. The observer will critique the interview and give suggestions to both the employer and the job applicant.

## DISCUSSION

1. Which role was the most difficult? Why?

2. What do you need to work on before you actually go for an interview?

## OPTIONAL ACTIVITY

Invite retired workers to come in to be the interviewers. Be sure to prepare the interviewers for the kinds of questions students are expecting.

# INTERVIEW

The more you prepare for an interview, the better you will do. There are two key steps: **find out about the employer** and **practice the interview**. Employers like applicants who take time to learn about the job and their company. You can learn about a company from:

- people you know who work for the company or who may know someone who works for the company;
- job postings;
- company publications; and
- references in library.

Appearance is important. Clothes should reflect those appropriate for the job. For example, if applying for a job as clerk in a sporting goods store, the job seeker might visit the store to see the kind of apparel commonly worn. The important thing is to be neat and clean.

Body language conveys who you are. Most people like a firm handshake with direct eye contact. Sit erect but relaxed. You should give the impression that you are confident of yourself and your work. Listen to the interviewer carefully and take cues from him/her.

An interview usually starts with a greeting and light conversation. If you were referred to this job by someone, this is a good time to bring up that connection.

Let the interviewer ask the questions. His/her time is valuable and you don't want to waste it with frivolous conversation. Here are some common interview questions:

1. Tell me about yourself.
2. Why are you interested in this job?
3. Tell me about any work you have done that would prepare you for this job. What are your strongest skills? How have you used them?
4. What would your teachers or employers say about you?
5. Describe your educational experiences.
6. What have you learned from the jobs you have had?
7. Why should I hire you for this job?

At the end of the interview, be sure to thank the interviewer and ask when you might hear from him/her.

After the interview, write a follow-up letter or make a phone call thanking the employer for his/her time. You may also use this opportunity to tell the employer something you might have forgotten to mention in the interview. Your follow-up gives the employer a reason to take another look at you.

SESSION 33:
# JOB-SEEKING SKILLS: JOB APPLICATION

## OVERVIEW
Students will learn about job applications and practice filling out one.

## DURATION
30 minutes

## OBJECTIVES
1. Students will learn about job applications.

2. Through practice, students will feel comfortable with job applications.

## MATERIALS NEEDED
Job Application resource sheet (copies for each student)

Job Application Form

## PREPARATION
Obtain real job applications in advance.

 ## ACTIVITY
1. Distribute and review Job Application resource sheet.

2. Have students practice filling out a job application. If real ones are not available, use Job Application Form.

3. Pair students to critique each other's job application.

## DISCUSSION
1. What did you learn from this exercise?

2. What do you need to do before applying for a job?

# JOB APPLICATION

The job application is an important part of the job-seeking process. Often it serves as the first impression that the employer has of the applicant. Every job application makes 3 basic statements about the applicant:

- The ability to be prepared and think ahead. When applicants walk into the office, they should come prepared with pens and pencils, information about themselves (relevant dates, credentials, etc.), references, names and contact information, and a résumé to clip to the application.

  *Note:* You should compile a list of references in advance. These should be people you have worked for and who can tell the employer about you. Teachers, former employers, and volunteer work supervisors can make excellent references. References from friends or family are not usually considered valid. Possible references should always be asked in advance if they are willing to have their names submitted to potential employers. If so, get their preferred mailing addresses and telephone numbers.

- The ability to follow instructions and to use accurate information. A vital part of any job is the ability to read and follow directions. Therefore, it is very important to fill out the application accurately. Follow these rules:

  a. Read the entire application before you start to write. Make sure you understand the directions in each section.

  b. Follow the directions exactly. If it says print, then print. Do not fill in sections marked for employer's use.

  c. Be honest. Incorrect information on an application can cause you to be disqualified for or fired from the job.

- The ability to complete a document neatly and to follow through on a task. A messy application may be seen as a reflection of the kind of work that the applicant will produce. Do not use such terms as see résumé, because the résumé may not be available at that point. If the question does not apply to the applicant, the correct response is n/a (not applicable).

# JOB APPLICATION FORM

## Identification:

Name: _____
        First                Middle              Last

Current address: _____

City, State, Zip Code: _____

A phone number where you may be reached: _____

Name and number of person to contact in an emergency: _____

## Job Desired:

Position being applied for: _____

Date available to begin work: _____

Salary or pay rate expected: _____

## Previous Employment:

Job title: _____

Employer: _____Phone/fax: _____

Address: _____

Dates of employment: _____Reason for leaving:_____

## Formal Education:

School most recently attended: _____

Address: _____

Phone:_____Dates attended:_____Degree or certificate:_____

**Activities (honors, clubs, sports):**

_____

_____


**References:**

Name: _____Address: _____

Phone:_____Relationship (employer, teacher, etc.):_____

Name: _____Address: _____

Phone:_____Relationship (employer, teacher, etc.):_____

Name: _____Address: _____

Phone:_____Relationship (employer, teacher, etc.):_____


**I attest that the information given on this application is accurate.**


Signature:_____ Date:_____

# SESSION 34:

# JOB-SEEKING SKILLS: ACCESSING THE JOB MARKET

## OVERVIEW

Students will learn different ways to access the job market.

## DURATION

30 minutes

## OBJECTIVES

1. Students will learn ways to access the job market.

2. Students will learn about the value of networking.

## MATERIALS NEEDED

Networking Diagram (copies for each student)

My Network (copies for each student)

## PREPARATION

Obtain real job applications in advance.

 ## ACTIVITY

1. Ask the students to come up with several ways to access the job market. This will probably include reading the classified ads; calling companies to see if there are openings; checking with appropriate job placement offices; using the Internet; etc. One of the most successful ways to get a job is through networking.

2. Distribute copies of Networking Diagram and My Network.

3. Ask students to define *networking* and discuss Networking Diagram.

## DISCUSSION

1. What did you learn from this session?

2. Can you name at least 3 ways to access the job market?

3. Which one do you think will be the most successful for you?

# NETWORKING DIAGRAM

THEIR FRIENDS, RELATIVES, ACQUAINTANCES, EMPLOYERS

THEIR FRIENDS, RELATIVES, ACQUAINTANCES, EMPLOYERS

FRIENDS

RELATIVES

YOU

PAST EMPLOYERS

ACQUAINTANCES

THEIR FRIENDS, RELATIVES, ACQUAINTANCES, EMPLOYERS

THEIR FRIENDS, RELATIVES, ACQUAINTANCES, EMPLOYERS

# MY NETWORK

You already know many people. The people you know also know many people. This can be your network to develop leads on interesting jobs. Chart your network by filling in names. Start with your family; then friends. Don't forget to ask former or current employers, teachers, people you have met in volunteer jobs, school organizations, etc., for help. As you talk to people about your career interests, ask if they know of anyone who might help you. Keep this chart and continue to expand it as you make new contacts.

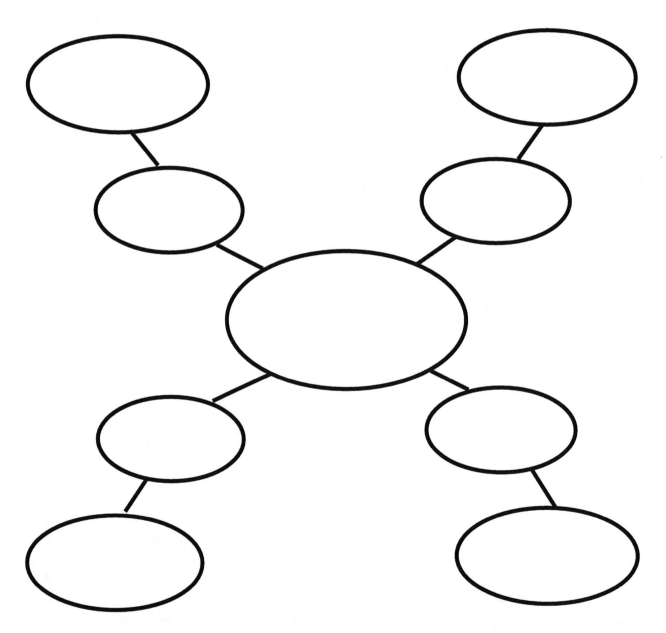

# SESSION 35:
# ACTION PLAN

## OVERVIEW
Students will bring all their information together and formulate an action plan.

## DURATION
30 minutes

## OBJECTIVES
1. Students will know how to plan and take action.

2. Students will commit to taking action on their plans.

## MATERIALS NEEDED
Focus on My Future (copies for each student)

## PREPARATION
None

 ## ACTIVITY
1. Read to the students:

   During this program, you have thought about your likes and dislikes, interests, skills, strengths, work values, and job availability. You have made preliminary decisions as to the occupation you would like to pursue. You are now ready to plan for the actions you must take—to Focus on Your Future.

2. Have students complete Focus on My Future.

## DISCUSSION
1. What assistance do you need to reach your goal?

2. What are your concerns now that you have reached the end of the program?

# FOCUS ON MY FUTURE

Write your goal below. What are you going to do and when?

**My Goal:**

_____

_____

_____

_____

_____

_____

I have worked out a plan for how I will reach my goal. The basic steps, in the order I will take them, are the following:

| STEP | WHEN |
|---|---|
| 1. | |
| 2. | |
| 3. | |
| 4. | |
| 5. | |
| 6. | |
| 7. | |

Once you have a plan, share it with someone else as a part of your commitment to carry out the steps. Find someone who will be supportive of your plans and who can encourage you as you go along.

I understand that this is my plan and that I have a responsibility to myself to complete it and to review and update it regularly.

Your signature: _____ Date: _____

I have shared this plan with _____ Date: _____

# SESSION 36:
# GRADUATION!!!

## OVERVIEW
Students will review what they have done in *Focus on the Future* and will measure their growth by taking the same test given at the first session. They are now ready to fill in the career plan that is a part of their portfolio. This may be done in class or at home.

## DURATION
40 minutes

## OBJECTIVES
1. Students will be able to measure their growth in their career development.

2. Students will be confident that they know how to plan for their future.

## MATERIALS NEEDED
What I Know About the World of Work (page 30) (copies for each student)

Career Plan (copies for each student)

## PREPARATION
Ask students to bring their completed What I Know about the World of Work from Session 1 to class. Have a graduation certificate for each student.

## ACTIVITY
1. Have the students retake What I Know About the World of Work. Have them grade their own papers. Ask them to comment on their growth since they first took the test.

2. If you want the students to fill in their career plan now, have them refer to the information in their portfolio. If you want them to complete it at home, explain that all the information needed is in their portfolio.

3. Ask for general comments about the program:
   - Name 3 things they learned about themselves.
   - Name 3 things they learned about the labor market.

- What do they wish had been included in the program?

- What part did they find the least helpful?

- What advice would they give to students just beginning the program?

4. Award students certificates of completion and tell them that they can take their portfolios home and use them in the future to plan their career moves.

# Career Plan

## PERSONAL INFORMATION

Name: _____

Address: _____

Phone: _____ Fax: _____ Date: _____

School: _____

Teacher: _____


## SELF-KNOWLEDGE

The important things I need to remember about myself as I make career decisions are the following:

1. _____
2. _____
3. _____
4. _____
5. _____


## WORK VALUES

My personal work values influencing my career goals are:

1. _____
2. _____
3. _____
4. _____


## CAREER ASSESSMENT INFORMATION

Key information from inventories and achievements that influence my career decisions are the following:

1. _____
2. _____
3. _____
4. _____

## CAREER EXPLORATION

I have discovered some of my likes and dislikes about career options as follows:

1. _____
2. _____
3. _____
4. _____
5. _____


## CAREER OPTIONS

Career choices that interest me are these:

1. _____
2. _____
3. _____


## CAREER DECISION

At this point in my life, I am interested in pursuing the following career options:

1. _____
2. _____
3. _____


The key factors in this decision are (interest, abilities, work values, lifestyle, earning potential, strengths, personal realities):

1. _____
2. _____
3. _____
4. _____
5. _____

## CAREER PLAN

I have worked out a plan for how I will prepare for my future. The following are the basic steps:

1. _____

2. _____

3. _____

4. _____

5. _____

6. _____

## TRAINING OPTIONS

To obtain the training I need, I will:

1. _____

2. _____

3. _____

## JOB-SEEKING CHECKLIST

When I am ready, I will do the following to help me obtain a job:

1. Ask teachers, employers, and other persons who know about my skills for letters of introduction and recommendation.

2. Update or prepare a new résumé.

3. Prepare a sample cover letter.

4. Prepare an application.

5. Register with a job placement agency.

6. Consider how I will get to interviews or job sites

7. Use my network to find out about job openings.

8. Contact potential employers.

9. Schedule job interviews.

10. Find out as much as I can about the employer/company.

11. Maintain a file for the employment inquiries that I have made.

12. Follow up all employment inquiries with thank-you letters or telephone contacts.

has sucessfully completed the

Career Development Curriculum

*Focus on the Future*

Teacher's Name

Date

School

# Competency Checklist for Unit Three

As a result of my participation in Unit Three, I . . .
*(Check those items of which you feel you have attained competency.)*

_____ understand the decision-making process.

_____ know how I make decisions.

_____ can use the career decision-making model.

_____ understand how change and growth can alter decisions.

_____ know the requirements for entry into my selected occupation.

_____ understand that there may be barriers to achieving my goal.

_____ have the skills to problem-solve ways to get around personal barriers.

_____ know how to construct an effective résumé.

_____ understand the importance of a good cover letter and how to write one.

_____ feel confident that I can participate in an interview.

_____ know how to fill out an accurate and neat job application.

_____ can name 3 ways to access the labor market.

_____ can chart my personal network of friends, family, and acquaintances who can help in a job search.

_____ can plan to achieve my career goal.

_____ have committed to take action to achieve my goal.

_____ can use the career development process that I have learned in the future as needed.

# A PARENT'S GUIDE TO CAREER DECISION-MAKING

*Dear Parent or Guardian:*

*Our children are entering a constantly changing and complex world. Therefore, it is important that we help them find direction so that they can make informed career decisions.*

*We have initiated a career development program that asks students to explore three major questions: Who Am I? (What are my abilities, interests, aspirations?); Where Am I Going? (What kind of work is available and what preparation do I need?); and How Do I Get There? (What is my plan for reaching my goal?). Families have a tremendous influence on the career decisions that young people make. Therefore, we want to involve you in the program and ask for your support and encouragement as your child participates in the various career lessons.*

*Occasionally, the school will send home announcements or ask parents to be involved in homework assignments related to the career development curriculum. The lessons are designed to create opportunities for children and parents to share ideas, opinions, stories, and concerns about the career decision-making process. We ask you to be open and honest with your children so that they can learn from your experiences.*

*This Parent's Guide to career decision-making is provided as a resource for understanding the kinds of messages that we are trying to impart to youth as they begin their career journey. Ask your child about the career activities and what is being learned. We hope you enjoy your involvement in the process. Please call us if you have any questions.*

# CAREER AS LIFE

We would like to propose that students consider their *career* as their *life*— not as just a job. Actually, people have five interconnecting life roles, all deserving considerable amounts of time, energy, commitment, and attention. The key to leading a successful life is finding the *balance*—but not necessarily equal time—among the following five life roles:

- **WORK**—finding occupations in one's life that provide satisfaction and sufficient income to meet economic responsibilities. The role of student is usually included in this category, but some people choose to see it as a separate life role, since lifelong learning is a concept that needs to be embraced to keep up with an ever-changing world.

- **FAMILY**—the choices that we make about having a meaningful family life. Conscious choices about choosing life partners, the size of the family, the kinds of relationships we want to nurture, and the special occasions that are celebrated are all ways that we can shape our family "careers."

- **CITIZEN**—the way we choose to participate in and contribute to our communities. Some people are actively involved in politics; some feel that paying taxes and voting on election day are about all they have time for in their busy lives; others serve on committees or find other ways to add to the health and welfare of the greater community.

- **SPIRITUAL**—seeking moral, aesthetic, and/or religious pursuits that help to "feed our soul." Some people even make this area their work role, but most people find a need to devote some part of their life/career to improving themselves and the world around them.

- **LEISURE**—the way we choose to spend our time when the rest of life's demands have given us a few precious moments of our own. This is the life role that gives us the most satisfaction, so if we neglect it, our physical and mental health may be adversely affected. Whether we engage in hobbies, sports, reading, or some other activity, leisure needs to be seen as a significant life role that helps us balance our "careers."

# STAGES OF CAREER DEVELOPMENT

Career development is a concept that includes all of a person's life experiences. Therefore, your career choices are often viewed as an expression of your self-concept. One's self-concept, and therefore one's career, tends to evolve through a developmental process. School is a wonderful place to begin looking at and learning from the stages of career development that we refer to as *Awareness, Exploration*, and *Preparation*. Experiences in the home can also complement this developmental process.

**Career Awareness**—Beginning at birth and continuing until our death (sometimes referred to as cradle to grave), we should remain open to discovering new insights about two major aspects of the career development process: awareness of self and awareness of the world of work. A major challenge for both educators and parents is to expand students' perceptions about the world of work and to promote an ongoing process of self-discovery.

**Career Exploration**—The exploration stage encourages individuals to investigate, try out, sample, experiment, experience, and make tentative choices about their career options. It is a time for eliminating options that no longer look good or feasible, and narrowing choices to a few solid alternatives that seem to offer the most satisfaction. It is also a process of seeking the balance that makes life rewarding. Ultimately, exploration leads to making career decisions.

**Career Preparation**—Once career decisions are made (and there will be many career decisions in life, not just one), a stage of preparation needs to be set in motion. This is a planning stage that creates a realistic path for achieving one's career goals. Sometimes the preparation involves education, other times it may involve technical training, and other times it may be a matter of laying out a detailed procedure for meeting all the requirements to get to where you want to go.

# THE IMPORTANCE OF DECISION-MAKING

One of the most difficult aspects of the career development process is decision-making. Many people are afraid of making wrong decisions, so they avoid making decisions altogether. Some people make quick decisions, then regret their impulsiveness. Others seem to trust their instincts but can't really explain how they make decisions.

We make decisions all the time: when to wake up, what to wear, what to have for breakfast, who we sit next to, which program to listen to on the radio, etc. Most of these decisions don't require a great deal of thought or effort. However, life occasionally presents us with some very difficult decisions, and those of us who trust our decision-making process are more empowered to make good decisions and take appropriate actions.

Many adolescents are facing critical, difficult decisions for the first time in their lives. As they move from a stage of dependence to one where they are asserting their independence, they need to have the skills to make decisions that will help them have confidence in their life choices.

Good decision-making involves the following factors:

- Being as specific as possible in identifying the decision to be made
- Identifying creative alternatives that provide choices for the decision
- Exploring the consequences of each alternative
- Identifying the personal values that are linked to the decision
- Identifying priorities
- Seeing the decisions in the context of other life goals
- Seeking support and feedback for the different options
- Making the decision
- Knowing how you will evaluate the quality of the decision

PARENTS AND OTHER FAMILY MEMBERS CAN PROVIDE ENCOURAGEMENT AND ASSISTANCE IN ALL PHASES OF THE DECISION-MAKING PROCESS

# Suggestions for Being Actively Involved in Your Child's Career Decisions

Our children are exposed to many influential people in their lives: peers, television and movie stars, teachers, characters in literature, political leaders, neighbors, and a host of other key players in their development. However, several studies have shown that parental influence is a major factor when students are engaged in the complex process of choosing an occupation and planning other aspects of their careers (lives). Schools and parents working together will create the most beneficial learning opportunities for students so that they can become empowered to make those critical life choices. Here are some significant roles parents can play in their children's career development:

- **Reflective Learner:** Share the lessons you have learned from your own career journey. If you were to do it over again, what things would you do differently? Highlight how even bad experiences have created good learning. Share the insights that have resulted from examining your values, priorities, and needs as they relate to career decision-making.

- **Role Model:** Children observe how we approach work tasks, our levels of commitment to our work, and the kinds of skills that we use to be effective in our jobs. They are also keen observers of parents' negative reactions to work and the effects of work on their parents' attitudes and behavior. Share what you like and do not like about your work . . . and why.

- **Information Source:** Children need information about the realities of the workplace. They also need to have the names of resources and people that can help them get accurate information to assist with their decision-making. Parents should provide their own network of friends and relatives as well as their knowledge of information-seeking tools that can assist their children in gathering up-to-date facts about the world of work.

- **Listener:** Listen to the dreams, the concerns, the hopes, the anxieties, the uncertainties, and the excitement of children as they talk about their futures. Listen to their decision-making process. Listen to their stories about jobs that they explore. Listen to their requests for assistance. Really listen.

- **Instructor:** Teach children skills that they'll be able to use for a lifetime in a variety of settings: communication skills, problem-solving skills, time management skills, negotiation skills, social and etiquette skills, organizational skills, proofreading skills, etc. Share the special methods or techniques that have helped you learn and apply these skills.

- **Opportunity Maker:** Exploration is a powerful tool in narrowing choices and making decisions. Seek out opportunities for your children to observe people in a variety of work situations, do job-shadowing, learn from computer programs, or participate in experiential learning about the world of work.

- **Stabilizer:** Assist your children in balancing their busy lives. Help them see that people really have five interrelated life roles as workers, leisurites, family members, citizens, and spiritual beings. If students have part-time jobs, then they really have two jobs. Setting limits (their own or yours) may help to create the needed balance.

- **Motivator:** The best motivator is showing interest in children's career journeys. Having high but realistic aspirations for your children helps them set goals of excellence. Encouraging their participation in school-based career activities reinforces the seriousness of the process. Pointing out the relevance of school experience when it is not obvious to your child will help maintain a focus on learning. Help children discover their talents.

# DEVELOPMENTAL ISSUES OF ADOLESCENCE

Adolescence can be a troubling time for parents and teenagers alike. Adolescence is a time for change, as teenagers move away from a childhood when they were dependent on adults to fill their needs and adults relinquish some of their authority and allow youth to assume more responsibility for their lives. It is a time for adjustments, as both parents and adolescents try out new behaviors and they create a different kind of environment that accommodates the changes.

Some major developmental issues with which adolescents typically contend are the following:

- Developing an identity—looking for a consistent, integrated sense of who they are as individuals

- Trying out roles that work in social and work situations

- Seeking independence—without losing connection to the security offered by past dependent relationships

- Risk-taking and experimentation

- Seeking approval—often from anyone who will give it

- Developing a sense of competence

- Integrating the many factors related to self-esteem

- Seeking comfort levels for daily routines and relationships

- Developing skills and attitudes that will provide a sense of individual power

- Achieving new and more mature social relationships

- Developing attitudes toward social groups and institutions

- Accepting their strengths and limitations

An awareness of these issues can help parents and families recognize some of the reasons adolescents seem to be struggling with their existence. Because they are normal teenagers, adolescents should be struggling a bit because the challenges facing them are significant. However, love, support, reasonable boundaries, and a good supply of common sense from important people in their lives can provide the foundation for adolescents to not only survive but to flourish in this time of tremendous change.